MILK BAR LIFE

MILK BAR LIFE

RECIPES & STORIES

CHRISTINA TOSI

WITH **COURTNEY MCBROOM**
AND SPIRITUAL CHAPERONE **PETER MEEHAN**
PHOTOGRAPHS BY **GABRIELE STABILE**
AND **MARK IBOLD**

Clarkson Potter/Publishers
New York

Library of Congress Cataloging-in-Publication Data
Tosi, Christina.
Milk bar life: recipes & stories / Christina Tosi.—First edition.
    pages cm
1. Cooking. 2. Desserts. 3. Momofuku Milk Bar. I. Title.

TX714.T674 2015
 641.86—dc23   2014041740

ISBN 978-0-7704-3510-3
eBook ISBN 978-0-7704-3511-0

Printed in Hong Kong

Design by Walter Green

10 9 8 7 6 5 4 3 2 1

First Edition

To the old folks who keep me longing to become a wise and weathered soul and to the young'uns who remind me to never grow up.

CONTENTS

INTRODUCTION

I'm not your average gal. I never wanted a pony, or to be a pretty princess when I was little. Instead, I dreamed of Cookies, Cookies, Cookies (working name), a bakery of my own that would leave me happily covered in flour and sugar, morning to midnight, and, if I played my cards right, an unconscionable amount of raw cookie dough. Chubby and sporting the finest bowl cut the local cuttery could trim, I would turn cardboard boxes into cash registers and bakery cases, practice making change with Monopoly money (you gotta know how to make the sale!), and concoct gluey batters and sprinkle-ridden doughs to feed to my stuffed animals (they were BIG fans). As I got a little older, my legs grew longer, and my dreams stretched too. I imagined a fun but simple place that brought people happiness and anchored their morning commute or evening stroll, a place where anyone could stop by, say hi, and eat cookies.

And, by some stroke of insane luck, universes aligning, honest-to-goodness hard work, and practical kitchen experience, that's exactly what happened. I opened Momofuku Milk Bar when I was twenty-seven, nearly six years ago. And in barely enough time to blink (and still not yet enough time to sleep) it has grown from one tiny bakery to a bigger thing than I ever imagined, all anchored by an 11,000-square-foot kitchen that sends cookies around the world and stocks six

shops in New York where people stop by, say hi, and eat cookies.

I can never quite put my finger on exactly how or why it all happened. All I remember is a onetime admission into the school of hard knocks, bakery edition. Dave Chang pushing me out of the nest and more or less tricking me into opening the first Milk Bar was also probably a big help too.

Funny thing is, when asked just how I got to where I am, I know the answer is pretty simple: I. Have. No. Clue.

When did it all begin? Shrugging my shoulders, I'll tell you it's always existed—I've always been working up to this moment. My entire life, all I have ever tried to do was to be me and stay me, Cookies, Cookies, Cookies and all.

Now I'm in it deep! There are more than ninety of us at Milk Bar, and it seems like there are more with every new batch of cookies that comes out of the oven. And, as the dream has grown, Milk Bar has turned into a huge family (that frequently drives each other crazy, just like any close family should). We blast bad music. We circle up overturned milk crates at 1 p.m. every day to sit together and eat family meal. We will all stop, drop, and roll whenever someone needs help, whether it's scrubbing down a station or nursing a broken heart. But it doesn't stop there.

This book is not just about food. It's impossible to separate the food and the stories behind Kitchen-Sink Quiche (page 151) or Mixed Nut Turtles (page 50). Each recipe exists in the smallest way because it's food and in the biggest way because eccentricities, camaraderie, and a don't-take-yourself-so-seriously mentality are the only way to approach anything and everything in life, including time spent in the kitchen. At least if you're living it on our terms.

Every moment we spend in the wild world outside the green double doors of our work is about the intersection of family, food, creativity, compassion, and simple acts of silliness and/or kindness. Cooking together, gathering for meals (even if it's sharing a candy bar for breakfast), and swapping food stories in the funniest scenarios are an important part of what keeps us full of smiles and innovation. We take road trips and have off-the-clock cookie swaps, beach days, and bingo nights; we even have a couple dozen beanbags hidden away for movie marathons, when we feast on nachos and snacks and act like we're thirteen again.

I think quirks are what make the world go 'round, just like dogs, dessert, quilting, jumping rope, bad movies, and great music. I love junk food. I play the ukulele. (More honestly: I take ukulele lessons.) I'd never sleep if that were possible. I would run for miles and miles every day just to be at peace if I had the free time. If I didn't live in New York City, I'd live in the middle of nowhere on a farm or a ranch. But I love what I do and I know how lucky I am. I get to choose to make a difference. Every. Darn. Day.

I am a dreamer. I want to create a world where cookies let people know it's going to be okay and remind them to let their imaginations run free.

These pages are my attempt to share that world, the Milk Bar world—the culture, community, and all-out sprint toward life through the food that surrounds and powers and guides our bakery and our lives.

Now let's get down to it: Despite the fact that many of us are formally trained and have worked in great restaurants, we also crave and embrace food with a more down-home, lowbrow approach. We long for FLAVOR, not fuss. There's no shame in saying I work fourteen hours a day and by the time I get home at 11 p.m., all I want is a SpaghettiOs Sammy (page 128) or something that incorporates eggs, cheese, and onions, the triumvirate that rules my hungry heart. *Milk Bar Life* is about celebrating it and not hiding it. (That said, I will take a meal at Eleven Madison Park any day of the week if you're buying.)

So I'm not trying to sell you a "got rocks," high-class, glossy magazine version of Milk Bar. We don't play that. This is how we really cook and eat—and with gusto because this food is just so damn tasty. I can teach fancy techniques as easily as I can teach simple techniques. It's about reading the situation and knowing what tastes good.

You'll find that the chapters are organized by my favorite occasions and inspirations rather than by course. That's how the day to day really goes, complete with Hand-Me-Downs, the dishes and desserts that I was raised on; Freakin' Weekend, when there's actually time to cook a big meal at home; Craft Night/Sleepover, when I need to feed my crafty mind with hijinks and freezer jams, complete with silly pajamas, *Die Hard* action scenes, and giggles; and Going Out, the days we wrap early, let our hair out of our colorful head scarves, put on something cute, and decide that hitting the town is the best way to shake off the workday and pay respect to our chef friends. Every chapter opens with a dessert, because, let's get real, behind every good savory dish, there's something else you *really* want to eat. I figured I'd make it easy for you, so you wouldn't have to go digging.

The lovely people who play any role, large or small, ALL inspire and enrich my approach to life, and so, I hope, I do yours. There is no end to this hilariously human, never tiring, wild ride. We are in charge and while curveballs are inevitable (well, not in T-ball), we get to choose our bat and then knock them out of the park. If you ever need a boost or a batch of Cornbake (page 30), or a Weak Night dining companion (page 117), you know where to find me.

CT 2015

HAND-ME-DOWNS

If the human body is 60 percent water, I'm certain that nearly another 25 percent of me is made up, bound together, and kept running by the recipes in this chapter.

For at least the first twenty years of life, my "culinary upbringing" was very honest and very delicious—and *very* not fancy.

I was raised by a gaggle of women who cooked and baked every meal for their families. Through food, they shared life lessons, hot gossip, and family histories. This was how knowledge and skill were passed down in the kitchen; no one ever considered honing her skills with culinary school or cookbooks—that wasn't what preparing a meal was about. Spending time in the kitchen was about feeding your family a warm, delicious meal (we're a picky, opinionated clan too), and just one of many things that has to happen in a day, so fussiness and complexity in a recipe never won a spot in the kitchen.

Cooking serves a specific purpose in any home. In my family, it's a rite of passage, but it's also a competition. We're show-offs, so not only do we want to make the most delicious recipe for our loved ones, we also want it to be the easiest (how else are we going to be superwomen the rest of the day?) and cheapest (frugality rules!), and have the best backstory (gotta have something to brag about when you're trying to stay humble).

Some people collect friends, or sweater sets, or fine art, or Beanie Babies. In my family, we collect honorary family members and we collect recipes—from in-laws, old friends, new friends, church folk, firehouse cookbooks, PTA potluck dinners, and eccentric neighbors. This is where you get the best stuff.

My family's culinary repertoire expands when a community gathering, new spouse, or cookie swap brings a new dish, a new recipe, into our orbit. I learned to cook and bake by making each of the recipes in this chapter as it was handed down and added to the recipe Rolodex.

The most honest, loving people make the most honest, loving food. It's not about fuss, it's not about exotic ingredients—it's about being resourceful with what's in the pantry. To this day, this is still what I home in on when cooking in my own kitchen, and the food I like to prepare, eat, and share most often.

In my "family," we cook and bake together, giggle, share, nurture, and feed others. Through these recipes, we teach new generations to cook and bake, to give more than just food. We make the tried-and-true dishes that decades of home cooks have made, the ones that are expected at any gathering. We hand these recipes down on index cards, or, more often than not these days, via e-mail, and so their legacy lives on. We remember where we got a recipe, who gave it to us, when we first made it, and how we may have tweaked it to make it our own.

Each of the recipes in this chapter is a staple in my life and in my extended, disjointed, glued-together loving family. Every recipe was handed down to me—and, now, to you. Share them freely.

MY GRANDMA'S OATMEAL COOKIES

— MAKES 1½ DOZEN COOKIES ——————

This cookie is the reason I learned to bake. There was always an ill-fitting lid on a beat-up plastic storage container in the fridge full of this dough, or a plate of oatmeal cookies wrapped in thrice-used aluminum foil on the table.

With great care, my grandma rolled every ball of dough in confectioners' sugar for a perfectly crackled finish, but she could never figure out why these cookies inspired the crazy in people. When he was away at college, my Uncle Dan would lie to his roommates and tell them the white stuff on top was mold, just to hoard a few more for himself. That was my grandma's favorite story to tell when she handed the recipe over to everyone who asked for it.

Though she would never go for this (it would probably get stuck in her dentures), I like to sneak some shredded coconut into the dough when no one is looking.

14 tablespoons (1¾ sticks) unsalted butter, at room temperature
¾ cup packed light brown sugar
⅔ cup granulated sugar

2 large eggs
2 teaspoons vanilla extract

1½ cups all-purpose flour
2¼ cups old-fashioned oats
1¼ teaspoons ground cinnamon
1¼ teaspoons kosher salt
1 teaspoon baking soda
½ cup sweetened shredded coconut (optional)

1 cup confectioners' sugar

1. Heat the oven to 375°F.

2. Combine the butter, brown sugar, and granulated sugar in the bowl of a stand mixer fitted with the paddle attachment on high and cream together until light and fluffy, about 3 minutes. Add the eggs and vanilla and mix until incorporated, about 1 minute. Add the flour, oats, cinnamon, salt, baking soda, and coconut, if using, and mix until just combined, about 30 seconds.

3. Put the confectioners' sugar in a small bowl. Scoop and roll the dough between your palms into golf-ball-sized balls. Toss in the bowl of confectioners' sugar until completely covered and arrange the cookies 2 to 3 inches apart on a greased or parchment-lined baking sheet.

4. Bake the cookies for 9 to 10 minutes, until golden brown and crackled. Let cool completely on the pan. For storage instructions, see page 47.

ROSEMARY NUTS

Back when I was a kid, I don't think anybody would have guessed that I'd end up a chef.

I was an infamously and annoyingly picky eater. I was more interested in arts and crafts and playing hide-and-seek than in food. Meanwhile, my older sister, Angela, was expertly adorning birthday cakes using a piping set she'd bought. She mastered a chocolate-orange ganache that she made into truffles, and she perfected these addictive rosemary nuts. She is now a stone-cold killer in the tech industry and, for some odd reason, calls me for cooking and baking advice.

I quadruple the recipe and bring it to work as a snack for our team, but there is rarely any left by lunchtime. Packed up in 2- or 4-ounce jars, these make a nice gift.

Before you get started, let me share a little nut know-how with you:

1. Invest in good nuts; please don't bring Planters anywhere near this recipe—preroasted, presalted nuts are absolutely not allowed here. (I have nothing against Planters; this just isn't the time or the place.) If that is all you can find, you're next to the popcorn and in the wrong aisle—look closer to the fresh produce!

2. I use a mixture of walnuts, pecans, almonds (whole or slivered), and pistachios. I typically steer clear of peanuts and hazelnuts because their flavor overpowers the rest of the mix, and cashews are hard to find these days at your standard grocery store.

3. Nuts *do* go bad! Store them in an airtight container in a dark, dry place, or refrigerate or freeze them. Taste-test your nuts before using them; if they taste "off" (trust me, you'll know if that's the case) compost them, give them to your pigs or chickens, or just plain get rid of them.

Now go forth and herb up the nuts.

---

1 pound raw unsalted nuts of your choice

2 tablespoons unsalted butter, melted
⅓ **cup packed** light brown sugar
3 tablespoons chopped fresh rosemary
2 teaspoons kosher salt

---

1. Heat the oven to 350°F.

2. Spread the nuts evenly on a baking sheet and roast for 10 minutes, or until fragrant and beginning to brown. Transfer the nuts to a large bowl (set the baking sheet aside).

3. Mix the butter with the sugar, rosemary, and salt, pour it over the warm nuts, and toss with a wooden spoon. Spread the nuts back on the baking sheet and let them cool on the counter for 30 minutes, or until all elements have solidified and cooled. Serve at room temperature. (They're not as good if you try to eat them while they're still warm.)

COCKTAIL MEATBALLS

— MAKES 2 TO 2½ DOZEN MINI MEATBALLS —

If you don't know, you better ask somebody.

These sassy little sweet-and-savory nuggets are nothing fancy until you stick a bedazzled toothpick in them. The totally '80s recipe is an easy share with anyone who has a Crock-Pot or a heart. My grandmother used to make these meatballs for the men at my mother's accounting firm during tax season, because they really "needed protein," and she would hand out the recipe to their wives once everyone was hooked.

---

1 pound ground beef
1 tablespoon kosher salt
½ teaspoon black pepper
1 tablespoon dried minced onions
2 teaspoons Worcestershire sauce
1 tablespoon whole milk
1 large egg
¼ cup plain dried bread crumbs

1 tablespoon grapeseed or other neutral oil

1 (12-ounce) jar or can cranberry sauce
1 (12-ounce) bottle Heinz chili sauce (don't worry, it's not so spicy)

---

1. Put the meat into a large bowl, add the salt, pepper, onions, Worcestershire sauce, milk, egg, and bread crumbs, and mush together until completely incorporated. Roll the meat into roughly 1-inch balls, about 2 tablespoons each, slightly smaller than a Ping-Pong ball.

2. Heat the oil in a medium skillet over medium heat. Depending on the size of your skillet, you may need to cook the balls in batches so as not to crowd the pan. Brown the meatballs, turning occasionally, until they begin to develop a crust, 3 to 5 minutes. You're not looking to cook them all the way through at this point, just to get color on all sides.

3. Transfer the browned meatballs, and any residual liquid or fat, to a slow cooker. Dump the cranberry sauce and chili sauce over them, cover, and cook on low for 3 to 5 hours—the longer the better—until the liquid has reduced to a sweet beefy glaze. (Alternatively, you can cook these in a covered saucepan over very low heat, but the Crock-Pot is how my clan does it.)

4. Put the meatballs in a bowl and skewer them before serving, or put a cup of frilly toothpicks to the side of the Crock-Pot for self-service. No matter what, serve warm.

Note that grape jelly, apricot jelly (a personal favorite), or any other jelly you might pair with beef works great as a cranberry substitution. And if beef isn't your speed, you can substitute another ground meat. Ground lamb and pomegranate jelly would make for a very modish and classy crock of balls. No matter which way you go, frilly toothpicks are a must.

SEVEN-LAYER SALAD

There's no better news than, when arriving at a lunch or dinner, hearing that seven-layer salad will be served. I ask for the recipe for every seven-layer salad I come across out of sheer curiosity. The best part about this kind of salad is that there are no rules as long as there are seven layers and the dressing involves mayo. In this regard, it's actually more of a seven-layer coleslaw. But in my neck of the woods, anything tossed in mayo is a "salad": ham salad, tuna salad, fruit salad . . .

1 cup frozen peas, defrosted
½ red onion, sliced
½ **head** iceberg lettuce, shredded
½ **pound** ham, sliced or cubed
1 cup shredded Swiss cheese
½ **pound** bacon, cooked and crumbled
1 ear corn, kernels cut off the cob

½ **cup** mayonnaise (Hellmann's, Miracle Whip, or Kewpie)
1 lemon, juiced
2 teaspoons kosher salt
⅛ **teaspoon** black pepper

1. Layer up the first 7 items, one at a time, in a bowl. Refrigerate.

2. Right before serving, after you have presented the salad to your guests in all its seven-layered glory, stir in the mayonnaise, lemon juice, salt, and pepper. Serve cold.

CHICKEN PUFFS

While I like digging through cookbook collections, I live for rifling through people's recipe card indexes. That is how I discovered this gem in my Aunt Sylvia's stash. Somehow this light and airy lunchtime favorite had fallen off my family's greatest hits list, and I can't for the life of me figure out why. I include it here to restore it to its lost glory.

Pam or other nonstick baking spray

¾ cup (about ½ pound) chopped cooked chicken
4 ounces cream cheese, at room temperature
¼ cup diced onion, scallions, or shallots
1 teaspoon kosher salt
¼ teaspoon black pepper

1 (8-ounce) tube refrigerated crescent rolls

1 cup Italian seasoned bread crumbs

Rotisserie or grilled chicken works best and packs the biggest punch of flavor!

1. Heat the oven to 350°F. Grease a baking sheet with the baking spray.

2. Mix the chicken, cream cheese, onion, salt, and pepper in a medium bowl.

3. Unroll the crescent rolls and lay out on the counter. Divide the chicken mixture evenly among the 8 pieces of dough, spooning it into little clumps in the center of each unfurled roll. Wrap the dough up around the chicken, pinching the sides to seal the seams. Roll the puffs in the bread crumbs and put on the prepared baking sheet.

4. Bake the puffs for 15 minutes, or until golden brown. Serve hot out of the oven.

HANKY-PANKIES

These misters are another retro offering that dates back to when my mother and aunts were the age I am now. I first loved them because of (1) their name and (2) the surplus of cheese in every bite.

They are more or less party-sized open-faced sammies crossed with meaty, gooey grilled cheese sandwiches. What more could you want?

½ **pound** ground beef
¼ **pound** bulk breakfast sausage
1½ **teaspoons** kosher salt
¼ **teaspoon** black pepper

¼ **pound** Velveeta cheese, chopped
¼ **pound** Swiss cheese, chopped
1 **teaspoon** dried oregano
½ onion, diced

16 slices party rye (such as Pepperidge Farm)

1. Heat the oven to 400°F.

2. Mix the beef, sausage, salt, and pepper in a bowl.

3. Heat a large skillet over medium heat. After a minute, add the meat mixture. Brown the meat, stabbing at it with the edge of a spoon to break it up, until no longer pink, about 3 minutes.

4. Meanwhile, melt the Velveeta and Swiss in a small saucepan over medium heat. Stir in the oregano and onion.

5. Add the browned meat to the cheese and stir until combined.

6. Put the slices of rye bread on a baking sheet. Assemble your hanky-pankies by spooning the cheesy meat mixture evenly over the bread.

7. Toast in the oven for 4 minutes, then broil on high for a minute to crisp up the tops. Be careful not to burn them! Serve hot.

SAUCE, WITH PENNE

— SERVES 4 TO 6, WITH LEFTOVER SAUCE —

I had a great childhood, not in a cookie cutter way, but because no matter which way my family went, we always lived in a house we called home, and we were lucky enough to have awesome neighbors with every move. I grew up with honorary grandparents and siblings and I added aunts and uncles every time I had a new address to memorize.

One of my favorite neighbors, in my tween and teenage years, was a Southern Italian family I routinely visited to play hide-and-seek and Super Mario Brothers, watch *Rocky I, II, III, IV,* and *V,* and, most important, to eat a second dinner. At home, we had fast food after softball practice, fish sticks on Fridays, or occasionally stuffed peppers (yuck! sorry, Mom), but my neighbors ate the same thing every night: bread and olive oil, then penne in red sauce, then beef braised in red sauce, and then salad. Their house always smelled of garlic caramelizing, beef browning, and tomatoes simmering to perfection.

Every day a fresh batch of sauce was begun again. The recipe had been handed down through generations on the husband's side to the wife, and when we were wise enough to realize we might not live across the street forever, my mom, my sister, and I begged her to teach us.

Whether you make this to freeze in batches and defrost, or make it fresh every night, I promise you will fall in love with its simplicity and that it will become a family recipe of yours too.

3 tablespoons olive oil
½ **pound** beef brisket

8 garlic cloves, lightly crushed
2 (28-ounce) cans crushed tomatoes
2 (28-ounce) cans whole plum tomatoes

kosher salt
2 pounds penne

½ **cup** grated Parmesan cheese, or more to taste

Cool leftover sauce before storing in a lidded container in the fridge for up to 1 week or the freezer for up to 1 month.

Time, temperature, and lid positioning are the secrets to this sauce. Medium-to-high heat, a time crunch, or too much moisture evaporation can lead to a mediocre, instead of awesome, sauce.

This recipe is correct! There is no salt and pepper, or any aromatic additives in the sauce, because they're not needed. Penne cooked al dente in salted water, with a garnish of grated good Parmesan cheese, will lend all the salt you need. You can, though, add crushed red pepper flakes as a sidekick to the Parmesan to add heat and depth.

In place of beef
brisket, any other
fatty cut of pork or
beef will do; boneless
beef short ribs or pork
sausages are a great
stand-in.

1. Heat the olive oil in a Dutch oven or other heavy-bottomed pot over medium-high heat. After a minute, add the brisket and brown it on all sides: This will take 10 or so minutes; do not rush it.

2. Throw in the garlic cloves and cook until golden brown, a few minutes. Add the crushed tomatoes. Crush the whole tomatoes by hand (wear an apron or a tie-dyed shirt for this task) as you add them to the pot, along with all of the corresponding juices from the can. Bring to a simmer and simmer gently over low heat, with the lid slightly ajar, for at least 3, and up to 8, hours.

3. Fish out the braised meat and put it on a platter to serve separately, keeping the sauce over low heat. Put a large pot of water on to boil and salt it like the Mediterranean. Add the penne and cook 1 minute shy of the package directions. Drain it well but not too well and add it to the pot with the warm sauce.

4. Season and garnish the sauce with grated Parmesan. Serve the braised meat after the pasta, with a little sauce, if you please. Make sure there's enough for that neighbor girl.

You can fill the acorn squash center with whatever strikes your fancy—breakfast sausage is my thing because it's sweetly spiced meat. The salt and butter ratios may seem high when you're dividing them up and seasoning the squash, but keep in mind you can't properly season all of the squash until it's time to dig in—so if you get bossy and cut down on either, your squash will be less tasty and fun to eat when you ring the dinner bell.

ACORN SQUASH WITH CINNAMON BUTTER AND BREAKFAST SAUSAGE

— SERVES 4 —

I wasn't just a picky eater as a kid—I was a picky eater into my twenties.

As I struggled over choosing dinner before dessert (most times dessert won), I met my match in a guy who embraced my ridiculous quirks (as I did his). He would search for *any* type of nonsweet ingredient I would actually eat, and if I expressed interest in a vegetable, a pasta, a meat, or anything that wasn't gummy or coated in sprinkles, he'd make a mental note and try to keep it in regular rotation on the dinner table.

Good men are usually raised by good men and good women. So once I met his parents, they hopped on the acorn-squash-is-a-vegetable-Christina-will-actually-eat bandwagon. This dish reminds me of their home, and I, in turn, cook it in my home when I need to be soothed or want to soothe someone else.

2 **large** acorn squash

4 **tablespoons (½ stick)** unsalted butter, at room temperature

4 **teaspoons** light brown sugar

1 **teaspoon** kosher salt

About ¼ **teaspoon** ground cinnamon

½ **pound** breakfast sausage, cut into ½-inch pieces

1 **cup** long-grain white rice

The "water bath" in this recipe keeps the squash moist when roasting. It also helps speed up the cooking time—just be sure to check the water level halfway through.

1. Heat the oven to 400°F.

2. Halve the squash and spoon out the seeds and stringy innards. Put the squash halves cut side up in a deep baking dish. Put the following into the cubbyholes of each squash half: 1 tablespoon butter, 1 teaspoon brown sugar, ¼ teaspoon salt, and a dusting of cinnamon. Add ¼ inch of water to the pan.

3. Cover the pan with foil and bake for 45 to 60 minutes, depending on the size of the squash, until fork-tender. Check the water level halfway through.

4. Meanwhile, sear the sausage in a medium saucepan over medium heat, turning occasionally, until browned, 5 to 6 minutes. Transfer to a plate.

5. Add 2 cups water to the saucepan and bring to a boil. (The leftover fat in the pan will give the rice an awesome sausage twang.) Add the rice, cover, and cook over low heat until tender, about 20 minutes, depending on the rice.

6. When the squash is done, pack its hollowed-out halves with the sausage and rice. Eat hot, with a spoon!

Feel free to add chopped onion scraps or any other miscellaneous veggies to the rice as it cooks. This is my favorite way to clean out the fridge when making dinner—I call it Rice Roulette!

CORNBAKE

— SERVES 8 —

My family is not Southern enough to make cornbread. Instead, we make cornbake, a spoon-bread marriage of cornbread and corn pudding. This recipe has been handed every which way in my family (there are at least two copies in every household's recipe Rolodex). It is the recipe I most often hand off to others. And it is implied with any invitation that I bring it as a side dish to any and all potlucks.

The old gals in my family make this recipe with more "supermarket" origins and will shout out the recipe when writing a shopping list (1 box Jiffy! 2 eggs! 1 tub sour cream! 2 cans corn! 2 sticks butter!). As much as I love that corn-bake, these days I prefer cornbake made from scratch. This "from scratch" version is so good it has even fooled the old gals in a blind taste test.

softened butter for the pan

1⅓ cups all-purpose flour

1 cup yellow cornmeal

3 tablespoons granulated sugar

3 tablespoons light brown sugar

1 tablespoon kosher salt

1 tablespoon baking powder

1 teaspoon baking soda

⅛ teaspoon black pepper

Serve this on its own or topped with crystallized honey and a sprinkle of salt. Or pour Cereal Milk™ over it!

1 (8-ounce) container sour cream

1 (14.75-ounce) can creamed corn

1 cup fresh, frozen, or drained canned corn kernels

½ pound (2 sticks) unsalted butter, melted

2 large eggs

¼ cup honey

2 tablespoons whole milk

½ teaspoon white vinegar

1. Heat the oven to 400°F. Grease a 10-inch round cake pan or a 9-inch baking pan.

2. Stir together the flour, cornmeal, both sugars, salt, baking powder, baking soda, and pepper in a large bowl.

3. Whisk together the sour cream, creamed corn, corn kernels, butter, eggs, honey, milk, and vinegar in another bowl. Add to the flour mixture and stir until just combined.

4. Pour the batter into the prepared pan. Bake until golden brown, about 45 minutes. Let cool slightly in the pan before serving.

AUNT MARY'S BREAD

— MAKES 1 (9-INCH) LOAF —

Most people don't make bread because they're scared of the process. Don't be one of those people.

My Aunt Mary isn't that kind of person: she bakes this bread all the time and brings it to every gathering. If it's lunchtime and I'm near her farm, I always make a point to cadge a sandwich at her place, because I know it'll be on a slice of this country-style bread. It has a little bite, a little funk, and a whole lotta sweetness, which makes it perfect as the star or supporting role for any meal involving sliced bread.

softened butter for the pan

3 cups bread flour, plus more if kneading by hand

2 tablespoons sugar

2 teaspoons kosher salt

Starter

⅓ cup warm water

¼ cup grapeseed or other neutral oil

2 tablespoons unsalted butter

1. Grease a 9 × 5-inch loaf pan.

2. Stir together the bread flour, sugar, and salt in a large bowl, then stir in the starter, water, and oil: Enlist the help of a stand mixer fitted with the bread hook, or roll up your sleeves, stir it all together with a wooden spoon, and then knead by hand. Once the mixture comes together into a ball, dial up the speed on the mixer and knead for 7 minutes, or turn it out onto a lightly floured counter and knead it until it's smooth and springy, no more than 10 minutes.

3. Form the dough into a 9 × 5-inch loaf and put it seam down into the prepared loaf pan. Cover with a slightly damp kitchen towel or a loose sheath of plastic wrap and let rise until doubled in size, 8 to 12 hours.

4. Heat the oven to 350°F.

5. Bake the bread for 25 to 30 minutes, until golden brown and a skewer inserted into the center comes out clean. As soon as it comes out of the oven, generously butter the top of the loaf. Remove from the pan and cool completely on a wire rack before slicing.

6. Wrap the bread well in plastic and store at room temperature for up to a few days.

I let my bread rise in the microwave (turned off) or my oven (also turned off) to create a temperature-controlled lair in which the magic can be made.

STARTER

MAKES ENOUGH FOR 1 LOAF

If you're a total bread dork, you can make your own wild starter in a moldy, spore-friendly basement. If not, the active dry yeast will help give your potato flakes a kick-start. (If this note scares you, ignore it and proceed.)

1 cup lukewarm water

½ cup sugar

3 tablespoons potato flakes

⅛ teaspoon active dry yeast

Combine the water, sugar, potato flakes, and yeast in a jar. Screw the lid on tight, shake to mix, and then leave out at room temperature for 24 to 48 hours, until the starter bubbles up, expanding into an amoeba-like state nearly twice its original size, and smells like a sweet, funky gym shoe.

CORNMEAL MUSH

I was raised with a Depression-era mentality: just because you don't have much doesn't mean you can't make something delicious. Cornmeal mush was a staple of my childhood summers and tax seasons (my mother was a busy accountant). It is essentially polenta or cornmeal that is molded, cooled, sliced thin, and panfried.

The original recipe called for cornmeal and water. I've churched it up a bit, though its appeal is really in the simplicity of its preparation and its potential to become the star of any meal, breakfast, brunch, or brupper.

5½ cups chicken, beef, or vegetable stock

2 cups yellow cornmeal
2½ teaspoons kosher salt
½ teaspoon black pepper

**OPTIONAL ADD-INS:
CHOOSE 1 OR MORE**

½ pound ham or cooked bacon or breakfast sausage, chopped
1 cup shredded cheddar cheese
¼ yellow onion, diced
¼ cup seeded and diced jalapeños

THE BREADING

1 cup all-purpose flour
1 large egg
1 cup cracker crumbs, plain dried bread crumbs, or all-purpose flour

4 tablespoons (½ stick) unsalted butter, plus more for smearing
maple syrup

1. Bring the stock to a boil in a medium pot over high heat. Add the cornmeal, salt, and pepper, whisking, and whisk constantly until the mixture comes to a boil. Lower the heat a notch and simmer, stirring occasionally, until the mixture is nice and thick—like freshly poured concrete—about 5 minutes.

2. Stir in your add-ins. Pour the mixture into a 9 × 5-inch loaf pan and refrigerate until chilled and completely set, at least 6 hours, or overnight.

3. Put the flour in a shallow bowl. Beat the egg in another bowl and put the crumbs in a third bowl.

4. Unmold the cornmeal and cut into ½-inch-thick slices. Dip each slice into the flour, then the beaten egg, and then the cracker crumbs.

5. Melt the butter in a wide skillet over medium-high heat. Once the foam subsides, fry the battered slices in batches, turning once, until they're golden brown on both sides. Serve hot, smeared with butter and drenched in maple syrup.

The add-ins are where your true personality gets to shine. The optional ones I recommend below are some of my favorites, but you can get baller and crazy and add caramelized onions (page 159), garlic (page 160), or leeks (page 160), or even stinky cheese and dried figs for a new take on a "classic" mush preparation. Also, a healthy splash of soy sauce in the stock never hurt anyone.

CHEESY ONIONS

— SERVES 4 —

These are expected at every holiday meal and family gathering. My Aunt Fran makes them best, and she handed down the recipe to me. Although cheesy onions usually arrive at the table in a casserole dish, cuddled in a decorative kitchen towel, like the precious gems they are, you can make them on the fly and serve them up in a saucepan as the side dish to any savory protein (which is how they most often appear in my apartment). Use any leftovers in Desperation Nachos (page 132).

10 ounces pearl onions, peeled

THE CHEESE SAUCE

2 tablespoons unsalted butter
2 tablespoons all-purpose flour
1 teaspoon yellow mustard
½ cup whole milk
6 ounces Velveeta cheese, chopped
2 teaspoons kosher salt
⅛ teaspoon black pepper

1. Put the pearl onions in a saucepan, add enough water to just cover them, bring to a boil, and cook until the onions are knife-tender, 3 to 5 minutes. Drain the onions and transfer to a heatproof bowl or small serving dish.

2. Make the cheese sauce. Melt the butter in a small saucepan over medium-low heat. Add the flour and whisk until smooth and the mixture comes to a boil. Add the mustard and do the same. Repeat with the milk. Stir in the Velveeta until melted. Season with the salt and pepper.

3. Pour the sauce over the onions and serve.

The same amount of any other onion—such as cipollini, Spanish, or Vidalia—cut into small (pearl onion–size) wedges will do here.

Fancify this dish by substituting 1 teaspoon Burnt-Honey-Mustard Dip (page 174) for the yellow mustard.

You can keep the onions warm in a low oven for up to 2 hours before serving.

APPLE DUMPLINGS

— MAKES 4 LARGE DUMPLINGS

My grandfather grew up next to an apple orchard, and when my grand-mother married him, she inherited dozens of apple recipes. This apple dumpling is *the* family favorite, and it's one of our ultimate symbols of love and care. While most of our hand-me-down recipes are one-bowl won-ders, not much to fuss or labor over, apple dumplings take more time and dirty a few more bowls and countertops. So when we bake them for you, the message is: you're worth it.

It's probably no surprise that my family tends to pick up old folks and fold them into the mix. When I was growing up, Zip, one of these fellas, had fallen ill. Deathbed ill, honestly, not that anybody wanted to talk about it like that. In my family, when we're at a loss, we bake. So each evening, my mother, after a twelve-hour day at work, would bake a batch of apple dumplings and take them over to Zip's wife, Penny. Penny would give the dish back to her the next day, and so it continued. My mother assumed they had visitors com-ing over all the time and shared the dumplings as such. She later found out that the dumplings were the only thing Zip ate for weeks, and the only thing that kept him going.

softened butter for the baking dish

THE DOUGH

2¼ cups all-purpose flour, plus more for rolling

3 tablespoons sugar

1¼ teaspoons kosher salt

8 tablespoons (1 stick) unsalted butter, cut into small pieces

¼ cup vegetable shortening

3 to 4 tablespoons cold water

THE FILLING

3 cooking apples (I like Granny Smiths)

⅓ cup sugar

1 teaspoon ground cinnamon

½ teaspoon kosher salt

THE GLAZE

1½ cups water

⅔ cup sugar

2 tablespoons unsalted butter, melted

¼ teaspoon ground cinnamon

¼ teaspoon kosher salt

This recipe scales up easily. The bigger the batch, the more you have to share. My mother always keeps disposable aluminum baking pans on hand to make sharing a cinch.

In some parts of the country, instead of a glaze, a can of Mountain Dew or Sprite goes into the baking dish. Though I normally take any excuse to crack open a can of pop, the family tradition stands here—a glaze from scratch is the only way to go.

1. Heat the oven to 375°F. Grease an 8-inch square baking dish.

2. Prep the dough: Combine the flour, sugar, and salt in a bowl. (You can make the dough by hand or in a stand mixer fitted with the paddle attachment.) Add the butter and shortening and mix until the fats are broken down to the size of peas. Add 3 tablespoons water and mix just until the dough comes together; if it does not, add the remaining tablespoon water and try again. Do not overwork the dough. Turn it out, pat it into a 4-inch square, and wrap in plastic wrap. Leave out at room temperature to rest.

3. Prep the filling: Peel the apples, core 'em, and cut 'em into quarters. Cut each quarter lengthwise in half and then slice the halves crosswise into ¼-inch slices. You want the slices thin but not paper-thin. Toss the apples with the sugar, cinnamon, and salt.

4. Make the glaze: Heat the water in a small saucepan or microwave-safe bowl until warm. Stir in the sugar, butter, cinnamon, and salt, and keep in a warm place until needed.

5. Unwrap the dough and, on a well-floured counter, roll it into a 14-inch square. (This dough is rolled thicker than your average pie crust.) Cut the dough into 4 equal squares. Spoon one-quarter of the cinnamon apples into the center of each square. Using a metal spatula, lift up the corners to meet in the center and press the edges of dough together to seal, with the apples sealed inside.

6. Put each apple packet in a quadrant of the prepared baking dish. Pour the glaze over the top of the dumplings and into the baking dish, filling it about three-quarters full.

7. Bake the dumplings for 50 to 55 minutes, until the tops are golden brown and the glaze has bubbled and reduced down to a syrupy consistency. Cool at least slightly in the dish before serving warm or at room temperature.

8. If the dumplings, for some strange reason, last for more than a day, cover the baking dish with plastic wrap and store at room temperature or refrigerate.

SOUR CREAM COOKIES

My Uncle Steve loves these suckers; and though I've never seen them in a fancy cookbook, or in the display case of either a high-end or down-home bakery, there's a reason they are in nearly every community cookbook I have flipped through in my Ohio family's various kitchens. While cakier cookies like this are very much *not* my speed (they're borderline whoopie pie–like), there's something about the intersection where the tang of the sour cream meets their fluffy texture that makes me unable to step away from the cookie tin once I've started.

---

6 tablespoons (¾ stick) unsalted butter, at room temperature

1 cup sugar

1 large egg

½ cup sour cream

1½ cups all-purpose flour

½ teaspoon kosher salt

½ teaspoon baking powder

¼ teaspoon baking soda

Sour Cream Glaze (optional)

---

1. Heat the oven to 375°F.

2. Put the butter and sugar in the bowl of a stand mixer fitted with the paddle attachment and cream on high until light and fluffy, about 2 minutes. Add the egg and sour cream and mix until incorporated, about 1 minute. Add the flour, salt, baking powder, and baking soda and mix until well combined, about 30 seconds. Though rather wet, the cookie dough is dangerously good at this stage—beware!

3. With a 1- or 2-tablespoon ice cream scoop, scoop the dough onto greased or lined baking sheets, leaving 2 inches between scoops. Or, if you don't have a small scoop, use a tablespoon, but work to make even, smooth scoops to mimic a scoop when dropping the dough, as the cookies spread and can end up looking super-messy.

4. Bake for 7 to 9 minutes for smaller cookies or 9 to 11 minutes for large ones, until the tops are golden brown. Allow to cool completely before removing them from the baking sheet.

5. If glazing the cookies, dunk the top of each cookie in the glaze. Or, if you're worried about getting your fingers dirty, use the back of a spoon or butter knife to spread the glaze atop each one. For storage instructions, see page 47.

SOUR CREAM GLAZE

MAKES ABOUT ½ CUP

Prepare the glaze just before you are ready to use it.

½ cup confectioners' sugar

¼ cup sour cream

Mix together the confectioners' sugar and sour cream in a small bowl with a spoon until smooth.

BUCKEYES

— MAKES 100 CANDIES —

Having parents from Ohio who were also graduates of OSU means celebrating the fine state's official tree, bird, and dessert in every way possible.

OK, I made up the state dessert part. But you are not *really* an Ohio native if you don't have these chocolate–peanut butter nuggets, fashioned to look like the state tree's fruitful "seed nut," in your fridge or freezer, or in the backseat of your car when en route to a PTA meeting or family reunion.

---

1 (16.3-ounce) jar Skippy creamy peanut butter

½ **pound (2 sticks)** unsalted butter, melted and cooked until slightly browned

1 (1-pound) box confectioners' sugar

2 teaspoons vanilla extract

1½ **teaspoons** kosher salt

1 (12-ounce) bag semisweet chocolate chips

2 tablespoons grapeseed or other neutral oil

---

1. Combine the peanut butter, butter, confectioners' sugar, vanilla, and salt in a large bowl and stir together until a smooth dough forms. Break off small chunks of the mixture (or use a 1- to 2-tablespoon ice cream scoop) and roll them in the palms of your hands to form small balls. Put them on a baking sheet lined with wax paper and refrigerate until firm, at least 30 minutes.

2. Melt the chocolate with the oil, stirring until smooth, in a microwave, or in a small pan over very low heat. Remove the balls from the refrigerator and, using a toothpick, dip them three-quarters of the way into the chocolate mixture, until they look like, well, buckeyes. Put the balls back on the wax paper to set completely, about 10 minutes.

3. Serve at room temperature or cold, straight out of the fridge or freezer. In a sealed tin, these will keep for up to 1 week in the fridge or 1 month in the freezer.

Browning the butter slightly will make the flavor even nuttier. If you really want to show off, brown the butter to high hell, and though your peanut butter centers will be a whisper less creamy, the depth of flavor will make people's eyes pop out of their heads in delight.

I'm all for using fancier chocolate in this recipe: anything from a 66% to 82% cacao dark chocolate will work well as a simple one-for-one substitution. But even the most stuck up of chocoholics won't be above eating these Buckeyes made the old-fashioned way, with just plain ol' chocolate chips.

A COOKIE A DAY...

Around the time that I was wrapping up college—where I studied Italian and mathematics—I realized something: I *really* didn't want to be a grown-up with a grown-up job. I feared regularity, repetition, and boredom. I knew myself, and I knew that whatever career path I chose had better be something I loved so much that I'd be willing to do it every day for the rest of my life.

And though it seems like a joke to type, or read, or say out loud, my course was clear: all roads led to cookies. I will never, ever, *ever* tire of cookies. I love to mix them, I love to scoop them, I love to bake them. And I certainly love to eat them.

They're the thing I turn to late at night at the bakery, what I relish making when everyone else has gone home, or when no one is looking. They are always exciting and new and never old.

From pizzelles to Linzers to pastelitos to animal crackers, whatever the cookie of your choice may be, I stand firm in the belief that, each and every day, we all deserve at least one cookie. (I err on the higher end. More like five a day. Thirty-five a week. One thousand eight hundred and twenty-five a year. This does not including tasting or eating cookies for work. That's work. The five a day are the for-me cookies.)

And, let's get real: bakers are some of the most competitive people out there. Everyone is on the hunt for just one more great cookie recipe, the new family favorite, something special for the upcoming holiday cookie swap or bake sale. Even my team at Milk Bar. Everyone wants to be the bearer of the best cookie.

This is a collection of my go-to cookie recipes, ones that I make on and off the clock. There are some stupid-simple cookies that wouldn't fit in with the cookies we serve at Milk Bar but are equally prized recipes for me. There are cookies with lemon in them and candy cookies that look like turtles. There are even a couple of gluten-free cookies in the mix, because sometimes the situation calls for them. Cookies are for every day and every occasion and what's the alternative—showing up without cookies? Bringing a *fruit plate*?

COOKIE LESSONS TO LIVE BY

I was raised and taught to bake by resourceful, loving, and *very* bossy women and many of these cookie "rules" came from them. Others are ideas from the overbearing family of ladies and men I bake with at Milk Bar.

cream	cake		cheesecake		frosting
pistachio	pistachio cake	pistachio milk	lemon curd	milk crumbs	pistachio frosting
pretzel	pretzel cake	chocolate stout	stout ganache	pretzel crumbs	burnt honey frosting
pineapple upside down	coconut cake	maraschino pineapple mix	P.U.D frosting	yellow cake crumbs	P.U.D. frosting
pumpkin pie	pumpkin cake	heavy cream + whole milk	brown butter graham cheesecake	candied pumpkin seeds + (pie dough)	pumpkin ganache
strawberry lemon	vanilla cake	lemon juice	lemon cheesecake	milk crumbs	pickled strawberry jam
carrot	carrot	heavy	cheesecake	milk crumbs	struesel buttercream

BUTTER: I make cookies with unsalted room-temperature butter unless otherwise noted. If you don't have time to temper the butter, add an extra 2 to 3 minutes to the creaming process so the friction between paddle and bowl can bring your butter up to a nice "room temperature" softness.

CREAMING BUTTER AND SUGAR: In this book, when I instruct you to cream butter and sugar, I'm asking for 2 to 3 minutes of paddling on high speed in a sturdy stand mixer. The cookie recipes in this book *do not* require the 10-minute creaming process that cookies in *Momofuku Milk Bar* do. Regardless of what you're baking, though, *always* scrape down the sides of the mixing bowl after creaming.

ADDING EGGS AND VANILLA: Beat for 1 minute on high until combined, light, and fluffy. Scrape down the sides of the mixing bowl.

ADDING DRY INGREDIENTS: I add mine all at once, on low. A 30- to 45-second mix is all a cookie dough needs. Scrape down the sides of the bowl. Then pulse the mixer on high speed 3 to 5 times just to be safe. No more mixing (unless adding a liquid). Tender, delicious baked goods depend greatly on mixing the dry ingredients *just* enough. Every additional orbit of the paddle toughens and tightens the dough.

MIX-INS: Pour them in 15 seconds into the dry-ingredient mixing, or fold them in by hand after the fact.

GREASING (OR LINING) BAKING SHEETS: Save the paper from your sticks of butter to grease your pans (or to press down your next batch of Rice Krispie treats). A can of Pam or other nonstick baking spray works if you're all out of butter

paper. Or you can make your own nonstick coating by mixing together 1¼ cups vegetable shortening, ¼ cup vegetable oil, and ¼ cup all-purpose flour. Store in an airtight container and apply with your fingertips, encased in a plastic Baggie, or with a pastry brush. Alternatively, you can line your baking sheet with a piece of purposefully sized parchment paper or a Silpat. Aluminum foil is not an option; it will conduct heat and burn the bottom of your cookies. As for wax paper, I'm paranoid that the waxy coating will bake into my cookies, and I don't trust it one bit.

COOKIE SCOOPING: Most of these cookies are drop cookies. I usually use a 2¾-ounce ice cream scoop for picture-perfect, same-size, big cookies; I advise buying one. A ⅓-cup measuring cup is a good cookie scoop alternative. Or you can roll the dough into balls in your hands if it's pliable enough. Unlike the cookie recipes in *Momofuku Milk Bar*, these quick-and-easy one-bowl doughs can go straight from scoop to baking sheet to oven, no refrigeration required. If your cookies don't spread as thin as you'd like, flatten the rounds of dough with the palm of your hand like you would a hamburger patty.

PAUSING: If you don't want to bake them right away, you can store the cookie nubbins in an airtight container in the fridge for up to 1 week or in the freezer for up to 1 month. Freeze on a baking sheet until firm, then put in the container. (My mom is the queen of this technique.) When ready to bake, arrange the balls on a baking sheet and leave out for 15 minutes at room temperature (whether out of the refrigerator or freezer), then bake away. Bar cookies, however, should be baked straightaway, but they can then be frozen once completely cool; defrost before eating. The Cookie-Dough Cookie (page 118) is a clutch move with a frozen cookie dough round.

COOKIE BAKING: Aside from properly mixing cookie dough, the other secret to success for cookies (and any baked good) is knowing when to take them out of the oven. Use your eyes (check the spread and color), ears (is that timer going off?), nose (does your kitchen smell like caramelized, buttery heaven?), and mouth (do you want them crispier?—add more time; or fudgier?—bake the next batch for less time).

Get in the habit of rotating your baking sheets from the top to bottom racks and front to back to ensure consistency. I like a fudgy center, so I pull my cookies out when they're clearly baked on the edges but still look a bit underbaked in the center. As the cookies cool, the centers will finish baking but remain softer and dream-like. The times that follow reflect my preferences; feel free to adjust for yours.

COOLING COOKIES: Cool cookies on the baking sheets. Cookies that are fudgy in the center do not move nicely onto cooling racks while still warm. Allowing the cookies to cool on the still-hot baking sheets will give them a sturdier bottom, making them less delicate once cooled. I put the hot baking sheets on cooling racks, not cookies on their own.

COOKIE STORAGE: *All* cookies taste best the day they're baked. It's better to make your dough in advance and then bake the day you're going to share or serve instead of baking the cookies themselves in advance.

Everyone has her own cookie storage preference, usually based on space constraints. That said, the best way to keep baked cookies tasting fresh is in the fridge, for up to 1 week, or in the freezer, for up to 1 month. Store cookies in an airtight container, by single cookie flavor (you don't want a citrus cookie commingling with a molasses-rye cookie), layered between sheets of parchment paper, plastic wrap, or aluminum foil so they don't smoosh or stick together.

If you're storing your baked cookies at room temperature, stick a slice of sandwich bread in the airtight container or cookie tin to keep the cookies fresh for up to 5 days. As the cookies begin to dry out, they will suck the moisture from the slice of bread and keep fresh, while the slice of bread becomes stale. This is probably the coolest trick in cookie-preservation history I know. I learned it from my grandma, who wouldn't be caught dead refrigerating or freezing baked cookies.

OTHER COOL STUFF

NONFAT MILK POWDER

Many of my cookie recipes call for nonfat milk powder, one of my favorite baking ingredients. It is easy to find in the powdered drink aisle, or occasionally the baking aisle, of the grocery store. Nonfat milk powder adds great depth of flavor, richness, and chew to cookies. Add it to any cookie dough if you'd like; usually a tablespoon or two will do the trick.

OAT FLOUR

Want a healthier, whole-grain cookie? Take old-fashioned (gluten-free, if desired) oats, throw them in the food processor or blender, and grind the heck out of them until they have a flour-like consistency. In recipes, you can substitute 1½ cups oat flour for every 1 cup all-purpose flour. (If measuring by weight, however, oat flour is a 1:1 substitution for all-purpose flour.)

MIXED NUT TURTLES

OK, I tricked you. This is not a cookie! But it'd be boring to open a chapter of cookies with a cookie, wouldn't it?! Plus, I count turtles as cookies in my cookie-a-day count.

My mother loves anything with caramel. One of my first food memories is eating Sugar Babies warm out of her purse (intentionally left there to soften on a hot summer's day). Turtles followed suit. Nutty and caramel-y? Sweet with a side of protein? She and I are *in*.

We learned to make turtles in culinary school, mostly for the caramelization technique, but I always wondered why they were made exclusively with pecans (not that I'm hating on them). If you're gonna get cheeky with a confection, why not really get some arts-and-crafts spirit up in the mix? The mixed nut turtle makes you feel a little kooky and quirky, like all good moments in the kitchen should, and is just a doorway into the animal life that a dollop of gooey warm caramel adorned with other pantry staples might take you. I'm envisioning a take on Noah's Ark for real extra credit points into my heart . . .

If you're feeling like a temperature ninja and/or are ballsy enough *not* to have a candy thermometer to do the job, test the caramel first by color—look for a nice auburn rust brown. Next, test the caramel's consistency by dipping a spoon into the caramel mixture and then into a little glass of ice water to cool it quickly. The cooled caramel should be firm and hold its shape but still have a slight chew—neither soft and super-tacky nor rock-hard crack.

5 cups raw unsalted nuts (I like almonds, pecans, and pistachios)

1 cup sugar
⅔ cup sweetened condensed milk
½ cup light corn syrup
6 tablespoons (¾ stick) unsalted butter
¼ cup water
1 teaspoon vanilla extract

1 teaspoon kosher salt

1. Heat the oven to 350°F.

2. Spread out the nuts on a baking sheet and toast in the oven for 10 minutes until fragrant. Cool completely.

3. Combine the sugar, condensed milk, corn syrup, butter, water, and vanilla in a medium 2-quart (or more) heavy-bottomed saucepan and cook over medium heat, stirring frequently, until the mixture reaches 245°F, about 15 minutes. It will rise up as it boils—do not leave it unattended or attempt to cook it in a small saucepan!

4. Remove the caramel from the heat and stir in the salt. Allow to cool on the counter until less runny (about 150°F) but still fluid.

5. Spoon the caramel into 1-tablespoon, gooey little pools onto a greased, plastic wrap–lined heatproof countertop (or other nonstick surface, such as a Silpat or nonstick sheet pan) and arrange 5 to 8 nuts in each to make funny-looking "turtles." If your caramel starts to cool down, return it to medium heat to warm until just fluid enough to continue making them reptiles.

6. The turtles can be stored for up to a week in an airtight container (they love moisture and humidity—beware!) at room temperature; separate the layers with wax or parchment paper so the turtles do not stick together.

Drizzle the finished turtles with melted semisweet chocolate chips to give them some stripes and personality.

If you want to play around with flours, like whole wheat or rye, reduce the quantity to 1½ cups, as heartier flours hydrate and bind differently than all-purpose flour.

If you want to bake up my childhood chocolate chip cookie, add ½ cup Rice Krispies and reduce the flour by ¼ cup, just like my Nonna used to do.

CHOCOLATE CHIP COOKIES

— MAKES 1½ DOZEN COOKIES —

I have a strong aversion to the idea of putting classic baked goods on our menu. I don't want to compete with your memories or your grandma; I want to bake things that she'd never think of but might love. But that's the professional me. When I'm at home, staying over at a friend's, or on vacation, I fully believe in straight-up celebrating the classics.

And when you're talking classics, nothing is better than a chocolate chip cookie fresh out of the oven. This is my go-to recipe. It's nothing fancy, just a stand-up cookie, crispy on the outside, fudgy in the center, with just the right amount of chew (brought to you by the addition of nonfat milk powder and the use of melted butter). And this cookie is great because you can make it by hand in one bowl, with a wooden spoon, just like the old gals used to do.

½ **pound (2 sticks)** unsalted butter, melted and still warm (not hot) to the touch

¾ **cup packed** light brown sugar

½ **cup** granulated sugar

1 **large** egg

2 **teaspoons** vanilla extract

1¾ **cups** all-purpose flour

2 **tablespoons** nonfat milk powder

1¼ **teaspoons** kosher salt

½ **teaspoon** baking powder

¼ **teaspoon** baking soda

1 **(12-ounce) bag** semisweet chocolate chips

1. Heat the oven to 375°F.

2. With a wooden spoon or sturdy spatula, mix together the butter and both sugars in a large bowl, flexing your biceps, until homogenous, about 1 minute. Add the egg and vanilla and stir until combined, about 1 minute.

3. Mix in the flour, milk powder, salt, baking powder, and baking soda until just combined, about 30 seconds. Add the chocolate chips and mix until evenly distributed, about 30 seconds. (If your dough is exceptionally wet, it's a factor of too-hot melted butter. Throw it in the fridge for a few minutes to firm up before baking.)

4. Portion 2¾-ounce scoops of dough 2 to 3 inches apart onto a greased or lined baking sheet. Bake the cookies for 10 to 12 minutes, until golden brown. Cool completely on the pan. For storage instructions, see page 47.

MAPLE PECAN COOKIES

My gal pal Karlie Kloss and I have been dreaming up flourless cookies since we started a line of gluten-free, dairy-free cookies called Karlie's Kookies™ in 2012. This cookie is a mash-up of a maple cookie we devoured from Whole Foods and a nutty cinnamon cookie we had been chattering about—and, like all of our collaborations, it's totally gluten-free.

1 cup pecans

3¼ cups almond flour
1 cup sweetened flaked coconut
2 tablespoons rice flour
1 teaspoon kosher salt
1 teaspoon cornstarch
1 teaspoon ground cinnamon

1¼ cups maple syrup
1 teaspoon vanilla extract

1. Heat the oven to 375°F.

2. Spread the pecans on a baking sheet and toast in the oven for 8 minutes until golden brown. Cool completely.

3. Put the almond flour, coconut, rice flour, salt, cornstarch, and cinnamon in the bowl of a stand mixer fitted with the paddle attachment and mix on low until combined, about 1 minute. Add in the maple syrup and vanilla, mixing until the dough comes together into a wet, sticky mass, about 1 minute. Mix in the pecans until evenly distributed, about 30 seconds.

4. Scoop and then flatten portions of the dough with the palms of your hands, like you would a hamburger patty, to make disks that are 3 to 3½ inches across and ½ inch thick. (Though delicious and cookie-like, these gluten-free babies don't spread a lick, so make sure to shape them into your ideal finished size.) Arrange 2 to 3 inches apart on a greased or lined baking sheet. Bake the cookies for 10 to 12 minutes, until golden brown. Cool completely on the pan. For storage instructions, see page 47.

HIJACKED BISCOFF COOKIES

— MAKES ABOUT 2 DOZEN COOKIES —

When I taste something good out there in the real world, I can't help but pick it apart, turn it upside down, and find a way to re-create it in my kitchen. These are my from-scratch, or "hijacked," Biscoff cookies.

Raise your hand if you don't know what a Biscoff cookie is.

Come on, people. I first encountered Biscoffs as the in-flight cookies on Delta. (I am usually the girl making a scene on the plane, begging for three more packs.) They're a variation of speculoos. Still nothing? OK, head to your nearest 7-11, because I recently saw them for sale next to the cash register. Actually, forget that. Just make these.

Biscoff cookies are the most delicious spiced shortbread cookie known to man, and they're slowly taking over the world.

If you're baking these for a festive event, you can roll the dough out ¼ inch thick on a floured surface and cut out shapes. Chill the shapes before baking. Time and temperature instructions remain the same.

1 cup all-purpose flour
2 tablespoons granulated sugar
⅓ cup packed dark brown sugar
1½ teaspoons ground cinnamon
¾ teaspoon ground ginger
pinch of ground nutmeg

scant pinch of ground allspice
½ teaspoon kosher salt
½ teaspoon baking soda
½ teaspoon baking powder

8 tablespoons (1 stick) unsalted butter, at room temperature

1. Put the flour, both sugars, cinnamon, ginger, nutmeg, allspice, salt, baking soda, and baking powder in the bowl of a stand mixer fitted with the paddle attachment and mix on low until combined, about 30 seconds. Add the butter and mix on low until just incorporated, about 45 seconds.

2. Remove the dough from the bowl and roll it into a log, 2 inches in diameter. Wrap in plastic and refrigerate until firm, about 30 minutes.

3. Heat the oven to 325°F.

4. Slice the dough into ¼-inch rounds and arrange 1 inch apart on a greased or lined baking sheet. Bake the cookies for 12 minutes, or until fragrant and dark auburn brown. Cool completely on the pan. For storage instructions, see page 47.

FRUITY-PEBBLE MERINGUES WITH PASSION FRUIT CURD

— MAKES ABOUT 2 DOZEN MERINGUES —

These sweet little things are a cheery, crisp yet somewhat chewy, rainbow-striped, bite-sized American take on Australian/New Zealand pavlova. They're also flourless!

4 large egg whites (cold and fresh)
¼ **teaspoon** kosher salt
1½ **cups** confectioners' sugar
2 cups Fruity Pebbles

Passion Fruit Curd

1. Heat the oven to 200°F.

2. Whip the egg whites in the bowl of a stand mixer fitted with the whisk attachment on high until fluffy, about 2 minutes. Sprinkle in the salt and whisk for about 1 minute, until the salt disappears and the whites stiffen slightly. Add the confectioners' sugar and beat until glossy, stiff peaks form, about 3 minutes. Whisk in the cereal until just combined, about 30 seconds.

3. Pipe 1½-inch rounds using a pastry bag fitted with a plain round tip or drop tablespoons of the mixture 2 inches apart onto greased or lined baking sheets.

4. Bake for 3 hours, until the meringues are completely dry. They should feel hollow and be slightly cracked. Let cool completely on the pans.

5. With a small spoon or the tip of a knife, hollow out the bottom of each meringue and pipe or spoon in passion fruit curd until it begins to creep out of the bottom. Serve, or store right side up in an airtight container in the fridge for up to a week.

PASSION FRUIT CURD
MAKES ABOUT ¾ CUP

Passion fruit curd is by far my favorite thing to eat with a spoon. Or layer into a cake, scoop into a pie shell, or stuff into meringues. Making a small batch of this liquid gold in the microwave is a cinch. If you are without microwave, poor you, cook the mixture in a small heavy-bottomed saucepan over medium-low heat, gently bringing it to a boil.

1 large egg
3 tablespoons sugar
½ **teaspoon** kosher salt

¼ **cup** passion fruit puree (found online and in Latin supermarkets)
6 tablespoons (¾ stick) unsalted butter, melted

1. Whisk together the egg, sugar, and salt in a microwave-safe bowl. Add the passion fruit puree and butter and whisk until completely smooth.

2. Microwave on high for 30-second intervals, stirring after each one, for 3 to 4 minutes until the mixture is thick and custard-like. Refrigerate for 1 hour, or until set, or transfer to an airtight container and refrigerate for up to 1 week.

SNICKERDOODLES

— MAKES 2 DOZEN COOKIES —

This cookie was a favorite of mine as a kid, probably because of the name. Putting the book together, I got to wondering, where does the name come from?

The *Joy of Cooking* (one of my oldest companions) says the snickerdoodle might be from Germany (makes sense, some of my kin are from there). Other sources claim that the name is just a made-up word in keeping with the New England tradition of nonsensical cookie names. I love them any which way, a slightly cakey sugar cookie rolled in cinnamon sugar. The cream of tartar gives them an awesome tang too.

½ **pound (2 sticks)** unsalted butter, at room temperature
1¾ **cups** sugar

3 **large** eggs
1 **teaspoon** vanilla extract

2¾ **cups** all-purpose flour
¼ **cup** nonfat milk powder
1½ **teaspoons** cream of tartar
1½ **teaspoons** kosher salt
1 **teaspoon** baking soda

THE CINNAMON SUGAR
¼ **cup** sugar
2 **teaspoons** ground cinnamon

1. Heat the oven to 375°F.

2. Combine the butter and sugar in the bowl of a stand mixer fitted with the paddle attachment and cream on high until homogenous, about 3 minutes. Add the eggs and vanilla and mix until just combined, about 1 minute.

3. Add the flour, milk powder, cream of tartar, salt, and baking soda, mixing until just combined, about 30 seconds.

4. Mix the sugar and cinnamon together in a small bowl.

5. Scoop the dough and roll between your palms into golf-ball-sized orbs. Toss in the cinnamon sugar until completely covered and arrange 2 to 3 inches apart on a greased or lined baking sheet. Bake the cookies for 9 to 10 minutes, until golden brown and crackled with the cinnamon-sugar coating. Cool completely on the pan. For storage instructions, see page 47.

RITZ COOKIES

It's no secret that I like buttery, salty, and sweet. This recipe is the paradigm of all things right in a cookie. I like to use these as a bread alternative to make a grilled cheese sandwich (à la the corn cookie sandwich on page 124) or dunk them into a bowl of tomato soup. I'm a grown-up, so I can eat my dessert and dinner at the same time if I want.

½ **pound (2 sticks)** unsalted butter, at room temperature
1¾ **cups** sugar

1 large egg

1½ **cups** all-purpose flour
¼ **cup** nonfat milk powder
1½ **teaspoons** kosher salt
¾ **teaspoon** baking powder
¾ **teaspoon** baking soda

2½ **cups (1 sleeve + 5)** Ritz crackers

1. Heat the oven to 375°F.

2. Combine the butter and sugar in the bowl of a stand mixer fitted with the paddle attachment and cream on high until homogenous, about 3 minutes. Add the egg and mix until just combined, about 1 minute.

3. Mix in the flour, milk powder, salt, baking powder, and baking soda until just combined, about 30 seconds. Add the crackers and paddle until incorporated, 15 seconds—you want them to break down into smaller pieces, but not cracker dust.

4. Portion 2¾-ounce scoops of dough 2 to 3 inches apart onto a greased or lined baking sheet. Bake the cookies for 10 to 12 minutes, until golden brown. Cool completely on the pan. For storage instructions, see page 47.

You can use plain, cheddar, or peanut butter Ritz crackers here—or any other salty soda cracker!

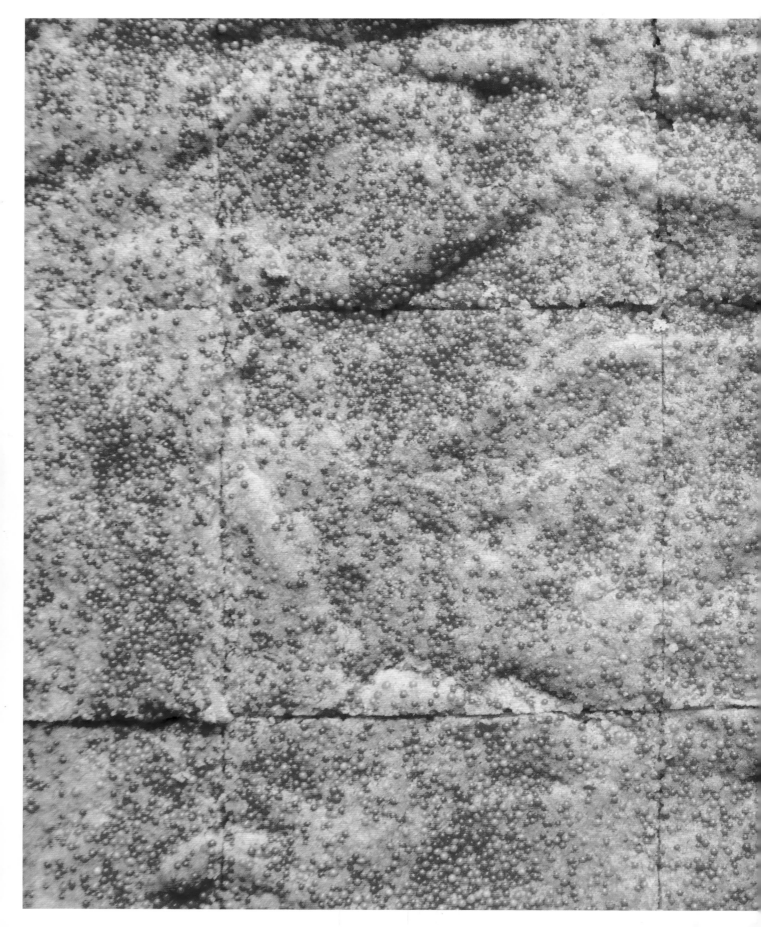

THE GRETA (SUGAR COOKIE SQUARES)

— MAKES ABOUT 2 DOZEN 2-INCH SQUARES —

I was raised on these sugar cookie squares. My fondest memories of them involve receiving disposable 9 × 13-inch pans of them once a week (that's 3.43 cookies a day) when I was away at college (and I didn't have a kitchen of my own to bake in). What a mom!

Even after I opened Milk Bar, my mom still sent me these sugar cookie squares, direct to the bakery. They became so legendary we called them "Greta cookies" or "the Greta," because you can't call a sugar cookie a sugar cookie in a bakery; it's just too confusing. Also, the difference between a sugar cookie and a Greta sugar cookie square is *huge*.

Their flavor is simple, but just as you think you're about to be under-whelmed, wham! You're hooked. Thanks, Greta.

Not a cinnamon sugar fan? Substitute any classic, radioactive, or themed sprinkle in its place to top the cookie slab just before baking.

½ **pound (2 sticks)** unsalted butter, at room temperature, plus more for the pan
2 **cups** sugar

2 **large** eggs
½ **cup** grapeseed or other neutral oil
1½ **teaspoons** vanilla extract

3 **cups** all-purpose flour
1 **teaspoon** kosher salt
1 **teaspoon** baking soda

½ **cup** whole milk

THE CINNAMON SUGAR
1 **tablespoon** sugar
1 **teaspoon** ground cinnamon

1. Heat the oven to 350°F. Grease a 9 × 13-inch baking pan.

2. Combine the butter and sugar in the bowl of a stand mixer fitted with the paddle attachment and cream on high until homogenous, about 3 minutes. Add the eggs, oil, and vanilla and mix until just combined, about 1 minute.

3. Add the flour, salt, and baking soda, mixing until just combined, about 30 seconds. Mix in the milk until just combined, about 30 seconds.

4. Spread the dough in an even layer in the prepared pan. Mix together the sugar and cinnamon in a small bowl and sprinkle evenly over the cookie dough.

5. Bake for 20 to 25 minutes for a slightly underbaked cookie (which is how I like it), or for another 3 to 5 minutes if you're a firm cookie fan. Cool completely in the pan before cutting into squares. For storage instructions, see page 47.

CITRUS COOKIES

— MAKES 1½ DOZEN COOKIES —

That's a *whole* lotta citrus in this here recipe. If you want to make a citrus cookie that tastes like you climbed up a tree and plucked a cookie off the branch, that's what it takes.

½ **pound (2 sticks)** unsalted butter, at room temperature
2 cups sugar

1 large egg
10 lemons, zested
4 limes, zested
2 oranges, zested

2½ cups all-purpose flour
1¼ teaspoons kosher salt
½ **teaspoon** baking powder
¼ **teaspoon** baking soda

Lemon Granola (optional)

Use a
Microplane or the smallest holes of a box grater to zest citrus. Use steady, even force, rotating the fruit as you zest and being careful to remove only the outermost colored layer, not any of the bitter white pith.

1. Heat the oven to 375°F.

2. Combine the butter and sugar in the bowl of a stand mixer fitted with the paddle attachment and cream on high until homogenous, about 3 minutes. Add the egg and all of the citrus zests and mix until just combined, about 1 minute.

3. Add the flour, salt, baking powder, and baking soda, mixing until just combined, about 30 seconds. Mix in the granola, if using.

4. Portion 2¾-ounce scoops of dough 2 to 3 inches apart onto a greased or lined baking sheet. Bake the cookies for 9 to 10 minutes, until light golden brown. Cool completely on the pan. For storage instructions, see page 47.

LEMON GRANOLA
MAKES 1 CUP

Add lemon granola to the mix for a chewier take, and the cookie becomes a lemon-tree-hugger cookie. When you hear that a cookie has granola in it, somehow you feel like you're making a "healthier" choice, right? Use Meyer lemons, a fragrant lemon hybrid more common in California than Brooklyn, if you can get your hands on them.

1 cup old-fashioned rolled oats
½ **teaspoon** kosher salt
3 lemons, 3 zested, 1 juiced
⅓ **cup** honey or agave nectar
3 tablespoons grapeseed or other neutral oil, plus more for the pan

1. Heat the oven to 250°F.

2. Toss together the oats and salt in a medium bowl.

3. Whisk the zest, lemon juice, honey, and oil together in a small bowl. Add to the oats and toss until well coated.

4. Spread the mixture evenly on a greased or lined baking sheet. Bake the granola for 25 to 30 minutes, breaking up clumps and tossing every 10 minutes, until caramelized. Let cool completely, by which point the granola should have become crunchy (it will still seem wet and mushy when warm). Store in an airtight container at room temperature for up to 1 week.

BANANA COOKIES

Never heard of banana cookies? Me neither—until about twelve years ago, when I was at wd~50 and asked Mike Sheerin, the sous-chef, what his favorite cookie was.

Most banana cookies are strangely cakey, like banana whoopie pies, because they are made with fresh bananas, and that affects their water content and texture. Personally, I like a fudgier cookie; a cakey-cookie person I am not. So I made up this recipe to suit my tastes, and Mikey's request, using banana extract and chips.

These cookies are great on their own, or as part of an ice cream sundae garnished with berries. Or dunked into some peanut butter or malted chocolate milk or coated in marshmallow Fluff. I know. I'll stop.

Banana extract is easy to find in the baking aisle of the grocery store.

½ **pound (2 sticks)** unsalted butter, at room temperature
1 **cup** granulated sugar
½ **cup packed** light brown sugar

1 **large** egg
¾ **teaspoon** banana extract

2 **cups** all-purpose flour
1½ **teaspoons** kosher salt
½ **teaspoon** baking powder
¼ **teaspoon** baking soda

2 **cups** banana chips

1. Heat the oven to 375°F.

2. Combine the butter and both sugars in the bowl of a stand mixer fitted with the paddle attachment and cream on high until homogenous, about 3 minutes. Add the egg and banana extract and mix until just combined, about 1 minute.

3. Add the flour, salt, baking powder, and baking soda, mixing until just combined, about 30 seconds. Mix in the banana chips until combined, another 15 seconds or so.

4. Portion 2¾-ounce scoops of dough 2 to 3 inches apart onto a greased or lined baking sheet. Bake the cookies for 9 to 10 minutes, until golden brown. Cool completely on the pan. For storage instructions, see page 47.

MOLASSES-RYE COOKIES

— MAKES 1½ DOZEN COOKIES —

I wanted to create a manly cookie, the urban-lumberjack, oversized flannel shirt of cookies, if you will. I kept having dreams of rye bread mushed into a cookie dough. So we recipe-tested the heck out of this guy, a marriage of a slice of rye bread and a gingersnap.

Saddle up and pair it with a whiskey, scotch, or, heck, rye, on the rocks.

---

8 tablespoons (1 stick) unsalted butter, at room temperature
1½ cups sugar

1 large egg
1 large egg yolk

⅓ cup molasses
1 tablespoon white vinegar

2⅔ cups all-purpose flour
1½ teaspoons baking soda
1½ teaspoons kosher salt
2 teaspoons caraway seeds
1 teaspoon ground caraway
½ teaspoon ground ginger

---

1. Heat the oven to 350°F.

2. Combine the butter and sugar in the bowl of a stand mixer fitted with the paddle attachment and cream on high until homogenous, about 3 minutes. Add the egg and yolk and mix until just combined, about 1 minute. Add the molasses and vinegar and mix until just combined, about 1 minute.

3. Add the flour, baking soda, salt, caraway seeds, ground caraway, and ginger, mixing until just combined, about 30 seconds.

4. Portion 2¾-ounce scoops of dough 2 to 3 inches apart onto a greased or lined baking sheet. Bake the cookies for 9 to 10 minutes, until a manly, leather-like brown. Cool completely on the pan. For storage instructions, see page 47.

THAI TEA COOKIES

— MAKES 1½ DOZEN COOKIES —

I wasn't raised on tea, but I love finding new and clever ways to get its flavor into baked goods, as is the case with this cookie. We originally created it for our friends at Band of Outsiders as a Fashion Week exclusive.

½ **pound (2 sticks)** unsalted butter, at room temperature
1¼ **cups** granulated sugar
⅔ **cup packed** light brown sugar

1 **large** egg

2 **cups** all-purpose flour
2 **tablespoons** nonfat milk powder
2 **tablespoons** Thai tea leaves (found at Asian supermarkets)
2 **tablespoons** instant sweetened iced tea powder
1¼ **teaspoons** kosher salt
½ **teaspoon** baking powder
¼ **teaspoon** baking soda

1 **cup** diced dried mango

1. Heat the oven to 375°F.

2. Combine the butter and both sugars in the bowl of a stand mixer fitted with the paddle attachment and cream on high until homogenous, about 3 minutes. Add the egg and mix until just combined, about 1 minute.

3. Add the flour, milk powder, tea leaves, tea powder, salt, baking powder, and baking soda, mixing until just combined, about 30 seconds. Mix in the dried mango, until combined, another 15 seconds.

4. Portion 2¾-ounce scoops of the dough 2 to 3 inches apart onto a greased or lined baking sheet. Bake the cookies for 9 to 10 minutes, until golden brown. Cool completely on the pan. For storage instructions, see page 47.

CUT-OUT COOKIES

These cookies remind me of my Nonna Trudy. In addition to Lemon Bars (page 170) and Chocolate Chip Cookies (page 53, always with Rice Krispies folded in), these were her signature dessert. During the holiday season, she would spend an entire week in cut-out-cookie production mode. She'd layer them between wax paper as she filled up tin after tin, stacking the tins like a bricklayer along the freezing-cold wall of her garage in Berea, Ohio. Then she'd wait for Christmas to arrive—or her chubby redheaded granddaughter to infiltrate her stock when dinner was done and the UNO cards came out.

The best part? You only need four ingredients. These cookies are my favorite greater-than-the-sum-of-its-parts foray into old-timey recipes and pantry staple ingredients.

½ **pound (2 sticks)** unsalted butter, at room temperature
½ **cup packed** light brown sugar

2¼ **cups** all-purpose flour, plus more for dusting
½ **teaspoon** kosher salt

Cookie Glaze
sprinkles

If you don't have cookie cutters, shape the dough into 2 logs, each 2 inches in diameter, cover, and refrigerate for an hour or more. Slice into ¼-inch-thick rounds, arrange on a greased or lined baking sheet, and bake.

1. Combine the butter and sugar in the bowl of a stand mixer fitted with the paddle attachment and cream on high until homogenous, about 3 minutes. Add the flour and salt, mixing until just combined, about 30 seconds.

2. Remove the dough from the bowl and form it into a ½-inch-thick rectangle. Wrap in plastic and refrigerate until cold, about 30 minutes.

3. Heat the oven to 350°F.

4. Remove the dough from the refrigerator, unwrap it, and dust with a sprinkling of flour. Roll it out to a ¼-inch thickness with a rolling pin on a floured surface. Using cookie cutters, cut out shapes and carefully transfer to a lined or nonstick baking sheet. (Work quickly; the colder the dough, the easier it is to cut, transfer, and bake.)

5. Bake the cookies for 8 to 10 minutes, until slightly golden around the edges. Cool completely on the baking sheet before glazing and decorating. See page 47 for storage instructions.

6. With a knife, palette knife, or piping bag fitted with a small round tip, outline or frost the top surface of each cookie. Decorate with sprinkles before the frosting hardens.

COOKIE GLAZE

MAKES ABOUT 1 CUP

I *love* using this glaze on pound cakes, muffins, and layer cakes in addition to cookies. Plus, the recipe takes all of two seconds. Make it right before you need to use it; it'll harden up if you make it in advance, though you can revive it with 5-second bursts in the microwave until it is zapped back to glaze state.

2 cups confectioners' sugar

¼ **cup** whole milk, cranberry juice, champagne, or other festive flavored liquid

food coloring (optional)

1. Put the confectioners' sugar in a medium bowl. Whisking constantly, slowly stream in the liquid of your choice until smooth.

2. Color the icing if desired. Frost away.

If you have rolling pin anxiety, shape the dough into 2 logs, each just a bit larger in diameter than your preferred cookie cutter. Cover and refrigerate the logs for an hour or more, then slice into ¼-inch-thick rounds, and use the cookie cutter to cut out a shape from each round. Place on a greased or lined baking sheet and bake.

Lightly dust an offset spatula with flour to make it easy to transfer the cookies from the counter to the baking sheet.

SALT-AND-PEPPER COOKIES

— MAKES 1 DOZEN COOKIES —

Sometimes I just want life to be simple: Black and white. Salt and pepper. A salt-and-pepper cookie! This cookie is great on its own, but it can go in many savory directions (like the Ritz Cookies; see page 59), and it is a force to be reckoned with when topped or sandwiched with Pickled-Strawberry Jam (page 210).

½ **pound (2 sticks)** unsalted butter, at room temperature
1½ **cups** sugar

1 large egg

2 cups all-purpose flour
1 tablespoon kosher salt
2 teaspoons black pepper
½ **teaspoon** baking powder
¼ **teaspoon** baking soda

1. Heat the oven to 375°F.

2. Combine the butter and sugar in the bowl of a stand mixer fitted with the paddle attachment and cream on high until homogenous, about 3 minutes. Add the egg and mix until just combined, about 1 minute.

3. Add the flour, salt, pepper, baking powder, and baking soda, mixing until just combined, about 30 seconds.

4. Portion 2¾-ounce scoops of dough 2 to 3 inches apart onto a greased or lined baking sheet. Bake the cookies for 9 to 10 minutes, until golden brown. Cool completely on the pan. For storage instructions, see page 47.

SUPER MARKET

I've always taken inspiration from the ordinary—especially the aisles of my neighborhood supermarket, where there's a world of everyday flavors just waiting to wow. Much like the hand-me-down recipes in the first chapter, supermarket recipes are based on ease, simplicity, and a resourceful knack, homing in on the spirit of creating something much greater than the sum of its parts.

I got into supermarket flavors because they were the easiest way for me to learn to cook and bake. As a kid, I didn't know any better (from a skill and technique or snooty highbrow standpoint), so I'd throw a few shelf-stable things into a bowl and whip up my own concoction. No rules: Just open, pour, and stir. This was around the time that home baking fads like making Rice Krispies Treats with any cereal but Rice Krispies was white hot, and happy home-maker shows were taking over the TV. Those were my culinary influences.

Now that I'm grown up, I know how to make all this stuff from scratch (I learned a lot from cookbooks and culinary school), but there's still beauty in the lowbrow brilliance of the supermarket way. I remember when my mom didn't have time to really bake something,

she would add some oil and an egg to a box mix and have a cake ready in minutes. In real life—outside of fancy kitchens—sometimes the thought and the motivation behind the dish are more important than making something that's technically perfect from scratch. And think about all the really good things at the supermarket: Have you ever tried making a Ritz cracker from scratch? Sure, it can be done, but the consistency and flavor of the store-bought ones are pretty damn impressive.

The recipes in this chapter reference my early years in the home kitchen, and include go-tos I still swear by to this day. I routinely prowl the aisles of the supermarket searching for flavor inspiration for my job in the professional kitchen or looking for something quick and clever to throw together at home in a jiffy.

RITZ CRACKER ICE BOX CAKE

— SERVES 6 TO 8 —

Ladies and Gentlemen, step right up and I'll show you how to magically turn three plebeian ingredients—grape jelly, Cool Whip, and a box of off-the-shelf crackers—into a delicious purple cloud.

Seriously, though, this cake *is* magic. It is a total transformation of ho-hum store stuff into an impressive and unlikely confection.

1½ cups grape jelly

2 (8-ounce) containers Cool Whip, defrosted in the refrigerator

1 (11.3-ounce) box Ritz crackers

1. Heat the jelly in a large microwave-safe bowl for 30-second intervals, whisking after each blast, until it is just fluid but not hot. (If the jelly is hot, set it aside for a minute or two to cool before proceeding.)

2. Whisk 1 cup of the Cool Whip into the jelly until the mixture is smooth. With a rubber spatula, gently fold in the remaining Cool Whip until completely homogenous. (This is how even the fanciest pastry chef incorporates a flavoring ingredient into whipped cream.)

3. To assemble the cake: Spread a very thin layer of the purple Cool Whip in the bottom of a pie tin or on a cake stand. Anchor in an even layer of Ritz crackers so that they touch each other but do not overlap. Top with a thick layer of Cool Whip (about 1 cup) and another round layer of Ritz. Repeat this process until the Cool Whip and crackers are used up and the tower is complete.

4. Refrigerate the cake for at least 4 hours, or, preferably, overnight before slicing and serving. Leftovers, should there be any, will keep in the fridge for up to a week.

Try another cracker, salty or sweet—saltines or graham crackers are also awesome in ice box cakes. Ditto for your favorite supermarket jelly flavors, if grape is not one of them.

PB CORNFLAKE NO-BAKES

— MAKES ABOUT 2 DOZEN COOKIES —

This recipe reminds me of those Rice Krispies Treats commercials from the early '90s—where the mom is pretending to slave away in the kitchen, but really she's just relaxing and having a grand old time because all she is doing is mixing together marshmallows, some butter, and a box of cereal. This recipe is just like that, only with peanut butter and cornflakes.

1 cup sugar

1 cup light corn syrup

1 cup Skippy creamy peanut butter

1 teaspoon vanilla extract

6 cups cornflakes

1. Combine the sugar, corn syrup, peanut butter, and vanilla in a large heavy-bottomed saucepan and stir constantly over medium heat until the mixture reaches a boil. Remove from the heat and stir in the cornflakes.

2. Drop 2-tablespoon-sized clumps (an ice cream or cookie scoop works best) onto a sheet of wax paper or a well-greased baking sheet. Let cool completely, about 20 minutes, before eating.

3. Store leftovers in an airtight container in the fridge or at cool room temperature for up to a few days.

Don't think twice about using a different nut butter or cereal in this recipe. Almond butter with Honey Nut Cheerios would be delicious. So would cashew butter and a mixture of Grape-Nuts and Chex. Let your imagination go wild! You may need to add up to a teaspoon of salt, depending on what the nut butter you use tastes like.

You can substitute honey, agave nectar, molasses, or any combination thereof for the corn syrup, though my preference is to go halfsies on corn syrup and anything else (even honey) so that the flavor of the sweetener doesn't dominate the finished "cookie."

CAKE-MIX COFFEE CAKE

— SERVES 10 TO 12 —

When I was a teen in Springfield, Virginia, the hot hotness in the *Washington Post* food section was a column called "The Cake Mix Doctor," an awesome guide to churching up cake mixes with select ingredients to create new-flavored cakes or cookies. Ground ginger! Ground cinnamon! Pecans! White chocolate chips! It was all the rage, at least in my mom's house.

When I worked as head baker on Star Island, off the coast of New Hampshire, Sarah Wicker, the head chef, taught me the power of combining sour cream and cake mix for instant, delicious coffee cake. There are two decisions you'll need to make before whipping up this coffee cake. First, choose the fruit you want to use. Then decide if you want that fruit canned, frozen, or in the form of pie filling. If you go with pie filling, you will spread it through the middle of the cake for a stunning layered effect. The other two options have you mixing the fruit into the batter, for a more uniform fruit-to-cake ratio. Any of the three variations will give you a scrumptious way to start, or end, the day. Serve it with a good cup of coffee, and get yourself in gear.

unsalted butter for the baking dish

THE CAKE
1 (15.25-ounce) box yellow cake mix
1 (16-ounce) tub sour cream
1 large egg

THE FILLING
1 (14-ounce) can fruit, drained
(I love peaches)

OR
1 (12-ounce) bag frozen fruit, defrosted
OR
1 (21-ounce) can fruit filling (such as cherry or blueberry)

THE TOPPING
½ cup yellow cake mix reserved from above
½ teaspoon ground cinnamon
2 tablespoons unsalted butter, melted

1. Heat the oven to 350°F. Grease a 9-inch square baking dish.

2. Prep the cake: Measure out ½ cup of the cake mix and set aside for the topping. Combine the remaining cake mix, the sour cream, and egg in a medium bowl and beat until just smooth, with no lumps remaining.

3. If you are using canned or frozen fruit, mix it into the batter and pour the mixture into the prepared pan. If you are using fruit filling, pour half the batter into the prepared pan, cover with the fruit filling, and top with the remaining batter.

4. Prep the topping: Toss the reserved ½ cup cake mix with the cinnamon and butter in a small bowl until the mixture is crumbly and streusel-like. Sprinkle it evenly over the cake batter.

5. Bake for 50 to 60 minutes, until the top is golden brown and a thin knife plunged into the center comes out clean or with a few traces of fruit filling. Cool completely in the pan before cutting into 2-inch squares and serving.

6. Cover leftovers with plastic and refrigerate for up to 1 week. If you have time, throw slices in the toaster oven to make something exciting and new for breakfast.

If you don't have
a 9 × 13-inch pan,
don't try to squeeze all of
the batter into a 9-inch-square
pan: You'll burn the top before
the filling sets; believe me, I've
tried. Instead, spread it into
multiple pans to get the same
level of filling, about
1 inch deep.

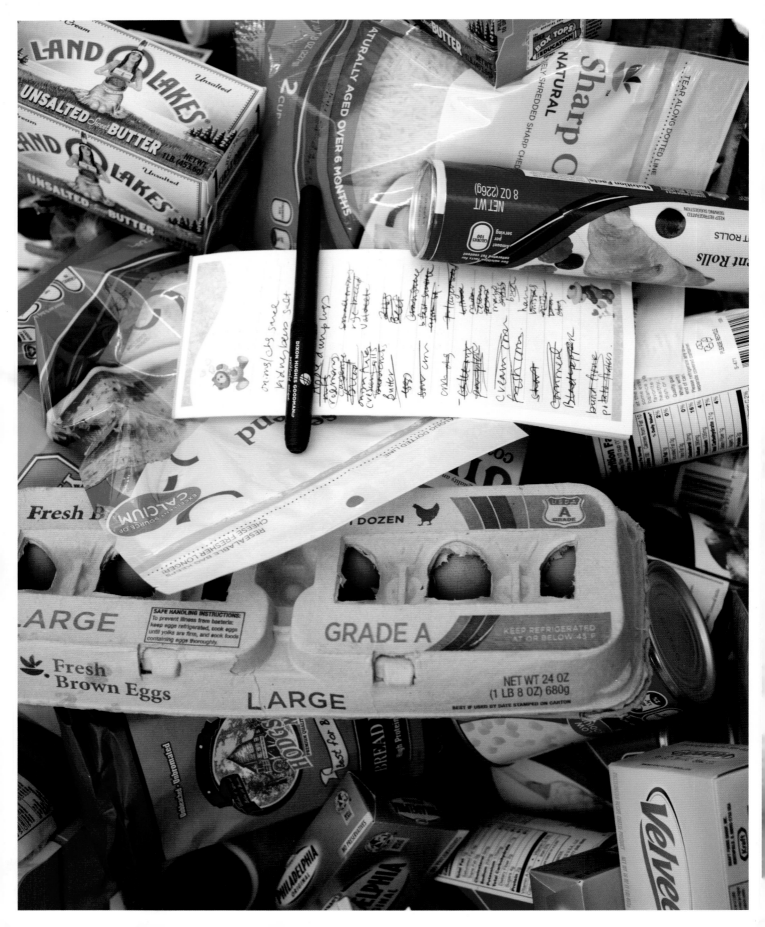

BEEF ROAST WITH GRAVY

— SERVES 4 TO 6 —

I love to imagine my mother, retro as all get out, leaving home on the farm, graduating from college, newly married, and trying to figure out how the heck to make some "nice" dishes for her man. She came of age in the "semi-homemade" era. When she was a young wife and a new mom, "beef roasts" helped her rule the roost. (She is a killer businesswoman, but she was also raised by a homemaker with homemaking values.) This recipe (so groovy!) was handed down from one of her sisters or girlfriends, and is tried and true, even to her kids and grandkids at the dinner table today.

1 (10¾-ounce) can condensed cream of mushroom soup
1 (2-ounce) packet dried onion soup mix
1 (12-ounce) can tomato sauce
1 (6- to 9-pound) beef brisket

1. Heat the oven to 375°F.

2. Mix together the mushroom soup, dried onion soup mix, and tomato sauce in a medium baking vessel, such as a 9-inch-square baking dish. Add the brisket and rub it down with the mixture.

3. Cover loosely with aluminum foil and roast for 2½ to 3 hours, until the brisket is ridiculously tender and the liquid has reduced and thickened (make sure that the foil is loose so some steam can escape and your soup and sauce have a chance to turn into gravy).

4. Transfer the meat to a cutting board, and let rest for 15 minutes.

5. Slice the brisket across the grain. Serve immediately, spooning the gravy over the top.

MANGO DRINK

— SERVES 1 —

Are you into the whole juicing, healthy smoothie thing? I'm not, but it's everywhere I look, so I can't help but have it seep into my neuroses. I don't have the time or money to jump on the juice bandwagon, though, so I've cleverly found a way to have a fruit smoothie morning, noon, or night: fruit sorbet mixed with other stuff from the supermarket. Am I missing the point? Maybe, probably, but my answer is tasty, quick, and easy.

Herein lies a recipe for three variations of a juice drink based on the time of day. All you need to do is go to the store and buy a pint of your favorite fruit sorbet. Now look at a clock and make the corresponding recipe. Though I won't tell a soul if you make the nighttime recipe in the morning.

MORNING

1 cup mango sorbet
1 cup plain yogurt

AFTERNOON

1 cup mango sorbet
1½ cups club soda
1 lime, zested and juiced
1 tablespoon honey

NIGHT

1 cup mango sorbet
1 cup club soda or tonic water
3 ounces vodka or gin
5 fresh mint or cilantro leaves

Combine the ingredients in a blender and blend for 1 minute, or until smooth. Drink up.

Do not underestimate the afternoon drink; it's actually my favorite of the trio.

I love mango, but you can use whatever sorbet you like.

WE ARE FAMILY

As is the case in most professional kitchens, at Milk Bar, family meal is an institution. Not only does it translate to "break time," it is also a Sunday dinner–like meal, where we sit in a Kumbaya circle, using milk crates as stools, and get a chance to enjoy each other's company and bad jokes. You don't miss family meal.

When Milk Bar first opened in New York City's East Village, we worked side by side with the cooks of Ssäm Bar in their underground kitchen, in the bowels of the restaurant and bakery. They made us family meal every day, which we happily scarfed down (we brought the dessert). When we moved to our commissary in Williamsburg, Brooklyn, a river away from any other Momofuku restaurant, we were forced to fend for ourselves in the family meal arena. This presented a great opportunity for us to roll up our sleeves and explore savory cooking on the clock.

And you know what? We *killed* it. Everyone takes a turn making family meal. Some offerings are a survival of the fittest exercise, making something imaginative out of very little. All are by far the most personal expression of cooking you can find in our kitchen. My favorite part is what you learn about each family member when he or she cooks. Every dish has an extraordinary backstory—it may be a feast from the cook's childhood, or dishes inspired by a cook's roots. It is honest, and loving, and delicious, like all good food.

When you knock family meal out of the park, you become a legend in the Milk Bar kitchen. Cooks who come on board years after you have moved on will get to know you through your jerk chicken. Or how you saved someone's hiney by turning what she accidentally overordered into a midday extravaganza that became a family meal gold standard.

Some of the recipes in this chapter are quick and easy, others are more involved, as the time available for family meal prep ebbs and flows based on how many compost cookies and crack pies we're churning out. Of the thousands of family meals we've prepared, these are our greatest hits, the food that fuels our creative minds and tones our hardbodies daily.

For those Milk Bar diehards out there, for ease of ingredient sourcing, note that I've substituted all-purpose flour for the usual freeze-dried corn powder here. Feel free to geek out and use the yellow gold instead for the realest of deals.

CRACKLE

— MAKES ABOUT 4 CUPS —

Because just about every moment we're not eating family meal together, we're making, tasting, or snacking on dessert, we rarely have dessert at family meal. But every once in a while we just can't help ourselves. That vat of crack pie filling waiting to be baked into toasted oat pie crusts stares you down, and you can't help but wonder, "What if . . ."

Crack pie® meets brittle = Crackle. It's a candy-like, mini version of crack pie filling, baked in a pan rather than a pie crust, yet just as addictive as its big sister. There's a choose-your-own-adventure aspect to making crackle: you can opt for your favorite flavorful snack food, or use up the end of a box of something that needs eating from the pantry.

½ **cup** granulated sugar
¼ **cup packed** light brown sugar
2 **tablespoons** all-purpose flour
1¼ **teaspoons** kosher salt

4½ **tablespoons** unsalted butter, melted
¼ **cup** heavy cream
2 **large** egg yolks
½ **teaspoon** vanilla extract

1 **cup** flavorful pantry item (cereal, crackers, chips, pretzels, snack mix, granola, etc.—nuts and seeds work well here too!)

1. Heat the oven to 350°F. Spray or grease a 9 × 13-inch baking pan, or line with a Silpat.

2. Whisk together the sugars, flour, and salt in a medium bowl. Add the butter, heavy cream, egg yolks, and vanilla and whisk until smooth.

3. Pour the mixture into the baking pan and spread it out with a spatula until ¼ inch thick. Crush up and sprinkle your selected pantry item over the mixture. Bake for 12 to 15 minutes, until dark brown (at golden brown, it will still be a little chewy, which is OK, but I like to get real color on my crackle). Let cool completely.

4. Remove the crackle from the pan and break it up into medium to small pieces with a meat pounder or a heavy rolling pin. Store the brittle in an airtight container and try to gobble it up within a month (or, try *not* to gobble it all up immediately).

LIL' Z'S ENCHILADAS

— SERVES 4 TO 6 —

Zoe Kanan*, one of our Texan transplants, started with us at the fresh-faced age of nineteen. She held her ground working FOH (that's *front of house,* or customer-facing staff, to you non-restaurant industry folks). She switched over to the BOH (*back of house,* or kitchen staff), moving up the ranks as a cook, all the way to Special Orders manager. If you've ever ordered a wedding cake from us, chances are she made it. Occasionally, if we were lucky, she'd step out of her role in Special Orders and fix us up some of her hometown specialties. Our fave? Her enchiladas, which disappear faster than a coyote in a sandstorm.

THE SAUCE
¼ **cup** rendered lard or bacon fat, melted butter, or olive oil
3 **tablespoons** canned Goya sofrito
3 **tablespoons** chopped fresh oregano
1½ **teaspoons** ground cumin
1 **tablespoon** chili powder
1 **tablespoon** unsweetened cocoa powder
1 **teaspoon** garlic powder
1 **teaspoon** kosher salt
½ **teaspoon** black pepper

¼ **cup** all-purpose flour

2 **cups** chicken stock or water
1 **cup** tomato puree

THE FILLING
1 **tablespoon** grapeseed or other neutral oil
1½ **pounds** skin-on boneless chicken thighs
kosher salt

½ **small** white onion, diced
1 jalapeño, minced
1 **cup** shredded cheddar cheese
1 **cup** shredded pepper Jack cheese
½ **cup** sour cream
½ lime, juiced
¼ **cup** canned crushed tomatoes
6 **dashes** Tapatio (or your favorite hot sauce)

THE ASSEMBLY
nonstick cooking spray
12 (4½-**inch**) white corn tortillas

½ **cup** shredded cheddar cheese
½ **cup** shredded pepper Jack cheese

¼ **cup** chopped fresh cilantro

I prefer dark
chicken meat to light. If you hate dark meat (though why anyone would ever feel this way, I'll never understand), you can use boneless chicken breasts here; just know you run the risk of overcooking the chicken and having it be a little bit on the dry side. To counteract this, in step 4, steam the chicken until it is just barely cooked through, about 4 minutes; it will finish cooking in the oven.

*Little-known fact about Zoe: She was an Olympic-hopeful ice-skating champ!

1. Heat the oven to 325°F.

2. Start the sauce: Melt the lard in a medium sauté pan over medium-high heat. After a minute, add the sofrito, oregano, cumin, chili powder, cocoa powder, garlic powder, salt, and pepper and whisk well. When the mixture is hot, whisk in the flour and whisk constantly until a smooth paste forms (congratulations, you just made a roux). Lower the heat to medium and, still whisking constantly, lightly toast the roux, about 2 minutes more.

3. Finish the sauce: Whisk the stock into the roux in 3 additions, whisking until smooth and emulsified each time. Whisk in the tomato puree until smooth. Remove the sauce from the heat.

4. Make the filling: Heat the oil in a large sauté pan over medium-high heat until almost smoking. Season the chicken thighs liberally on both sides with salt. Lay the chicken thighs skin side down in the pan and sear them until they're browned on the first side, 3 to 5 minutes—they'll be ready to flip when they release easily from the pan. Flip them and cook for a minute or so, then add enough water to the pan to come about ¼ inch up the sides of the chicken. Once the water boils, reduce the heat so it simmers, cover the pan, and steam the chicken until just cooked through; it shouldn't take longer than 10 minutes. Transfer the chicken to a bowl and let cool. Reserve ¼ cup of the cooking liquid, and scrape all the browned-meat goodness off the bottom of the pan; reserve it with the liquid.

5. Once it is cool enough to handle, shred the chicken, transfer to a bowl, and toss with the onion, jalapeño, cheeses, sour cream, lime juice, crushed tomatoes, 1 teaspoon salt, the reserved cooking liquid, and hot sauce.

6. Grease a 9 × 13-inch glass baking dish. Spread ½ cup of the enchilada sauce over the bottom.

7. Set a sauté pan over medium heat and spray it liberally with nonstick spray. One at a time, heat the tortillas, turning once, until flexible, about 30 seconds per side. As you soften them, stack the tortillas on a plate with another plate inverted on top to keep them warm and pliable.

8. Assemble the enchiladas: Spoon a tightly packed ¼ cup of filling onto a tortilla. Use your hands to mold the filling into a compact cigar shape running the length of the tortilla. Roll the tortilla up around the filling and place seam side down in the baking dish, anchoring it in the sauce layer. Repeat with the rest of the tortillas and filling. Scrunch the enchiladas together if you need to; they will all fit in the dish.

9. Spread the remaining sauce over the top of the enchiladas and cover them with the cheeses.

10. Bake for 15 minutes, or until the sauce begins to bubble up and the cheese is melted and just beginning to brown around the edges. Let cool for 10 minutes.

11. Sprinkle the top of the enchiladas with the chopped cilantro before serving.

HAUTE DOGS

— MAKES 8 DOGS; SERVES 4 TO 6 —

This recipe is a result of Fourth of July ordering gone awry (read: someone ordered *way* too many hot dogs). They're like pigs in a blanket, except with hot dogs and condiments wrapped inside freshly baked dough. They are great for children and excellent for fueling hungry cooks. So good, so easy, so haute.

The Milk Bar
crew's most-loved fixins are ketchup, mustard, Burnt-Honey-Mustard Dip (page 174), chopped onions, Caramelized Onions (page 159), Sweet-and-Sour Red Onion Jam (page 215), Bean Dip (page 174), cheese sticks, kimchi, peppers, relish, chili, and Fritos. Or whatever floats your boat. The secret is putting them in with the rolled dogs before baking, as opposed to garnishing or dunking after the fact.

THE DOUGH

3 cups all-purpose flour
1 tablespoon kosher salt
½ (¼-ounce) packet active dry yeast
1¾ cups warm water

8 hot dogs
fixins

THE EGG WASH

1 egg
½ teaspoon water

2 tablespoons sesame or poppy seeds

1. Make the dough: Stir together the flour, salt, and yeast in the bowl of a stand mixer—do it by hand, using the dough hook like a spoon. Continue stirring by hand as you add the water, until the mixture has come together in a shaggy mass.

2. Engage the bowl and hook and mix the dough on the lowest speed for 3 minutes, or until it is somewhat smooth and cohesive. Knead for 4 more minutes on the lowest speed. The dough should look like a wet ball and bounce back softly when prodded.

3. Film a large bowl with oil and dump the dough into it. Cover with plastic wrap and let the dough proof overnight in the fridge.

4. The next day, when you're ready to bake, heat the oven to 350°F. Divide the dough into 8 equal pieces. Roll out each one into a rectangle roughly the length of a hot dog and wide enough to fully wrap around the dog, about 8 by 5 inches.

5. Spread the dough with any combination of fixins. Put a hot dog on top of each piece of dough and wrap up like a baby in a blanket. Put the dough-wrapped dogs seam side down on a greased or parchment-lined baking sheet.

6. Make the egg wash: Use a fork to whisk together the egg and water in a small bowl. Brush each blanketed dog with egg wash and sprinkle with some sesame seeds.

7. Bake for 20 minutes, or until the bread blankets puff slightly and take on a golden hue. Eat hot or at room temperature.

TEX-MEX CURRIED CHILI WITH AVOCADO RAITA

— SERVES 4 TO 6 —

Tex-Mex and curry are Courtney McBroom's two favorite types of food, and this dish, which incorporates both of them, quickly became a weekly family meal standard after she shared it with us. The list of ingredients may be long (half are spices) but the effort in opening up and properly measuring each spice is worth it.

3 **tablespoons** chili powder
2 **teaspoons** ground cumin
2 **teaspoons** yellow curry powder
2 **teaspoons** turmeric
1 **teaspoon** garam masala
1 **teaspoon** dried oregano
½ **teaspoon** cayenne pepper
¼ **teaspoon** ground cinnamon
¼ **teaspoon** ground coriander

3 **tablespoons** grapeseed or other neutral oil

2 **medium** carrots, peeled and diced
2 **small** white onions, diced
1 jalapeño, chopped (with seeds)

1 **tablespoon** finely chopped peeled fresh ginger
4 garlic cloves, finely chopped
kosher salt

¼ **cup** tomato paste

2 limes, juiced, rinds reserved
¼ **cup** white vinegar

2 **pounds** lean ground beef

2 **cups** chicken stock
2 **(13-ounce) cans** unsweetened coconut milk

¼ **cup** chopped fresh cilantro
Avocado Raita (page 98)

1. Mix together the chili powder, cumin, curry powder, turmeric, garam masala, oregano, cayenne, cinnamon, and coriander in a small bowl.

2. Heat the oil in a heavy-bottomed stockpot over medium-high heat until hot. Add the spice mix and toast, stirring constantly with a heatproof spatula, until fragrant, about 2 minutes.

3. Add the carrots, onions, jalapeño, ginger, garlic, and ½ teaspoon salt, stirring to coat everything in the toasted spice mixture, then reduce the heat to medium-low and cook until the vegetables soften and their volume decreases by at least half, about 15 minutes.

4. Stir in the tomato paste and cook until fragrant, another 2 to 3 minutes. Add the lime juice and vinegar and bring to a simmer.

(recipe continues)

5. Add the ground beef and 2½ teaspoons salt and cook, stirring often and using the spatula or a wooden spoon to break the meat down into small bits and scrape the browned bits off the bottom of the pot, until the meat is caramelized, coated in spice, and cooked through, about 10 minutes.

6. Add the chicken stock, coconut milk, and lime rinds, scrape the bottom of the pot again, and bring the liquid to a boil. Reduce the heat so it simmers and cook, uncovered, until the liquid reduces by half, about 45 minutes. Stir it every once in a while so the bottom doesn't burn.

7. Once the chili is at your approved thickness, remove the lime rinds and taste it for salt and add more if you think it needs it. Serve it in bowls and top it with the cilantro and avocado raita.

AVOCADO RAITA
SERVES 4 TO 6

Guacamole meets cucumber raita. Tex-Mex meets Indian. This is without a doubt the most important part of the chili recipe. Don't even think about making the chili if you aren't going to make the raita; it'd be as sinful as shorting a bowl of American-style chili its God-given right to a dollop of sour cream.

1 ripe avocado

1 lime, juiced

½ English cucumber, peeled and diced
2 scallions, thinly sliced
1 jalapeño, diced (with seeds if you like it hot)

½ **cup** plain yogurt
½ **cup** sour cream
½ **teaspoon** light brown sugar
1 teaspoon kosher salt

1. Split the avocado in half and remove and discard the pit. With the tip of a sharp knife, cut a grid into the flesh of each half. Use a spoon to scrape the cubes out of the avocado and into a medium bowl. Pour the lime juice over the cubed avocado and give it a stir. (This prevents the avocado from browning.)

2. Add the cucumber, scallions, and jalapeño to the avocado and stir it up.

3. Whisk together the yogurt, sour cream, brown sugar, and salt in a small bowl until smooth. Pour over the avocado mixture and stir. Serve immediately.

EGGS IN PURGATORY

This was the signature family meal of Heather Pelletier, one of our OG cooks. In its most basic form, it is simply eggs poached in tomato sauce. However, we've souped it up on occasion with a few extra ingredients, and you're getting the souped-up version here. Even though Heather is long gone from Milk Bar, her eggs in purgatory still holds sway as one of our most prized family meal creations, easy to whip up on the fly when the clock strikes 12:45 and we need something warm and delicious *fast*!

For an all-out, baller eggs-in-purgatory meal, source local, farm fresh eggs. Trust me, it really does make a difference.

2 tablespoons olive oil

½ **medium** Spanish onion, minced

3 garlic cloves, minced

½ **teaspoon** crushed red pepper flakes

1 (28-ounce) can whole peeled tomatoes, crushed by hand, with their liquid

1 teaspoon kosher salt

1 teaspoon sugar

1 teaspoon sherry vinegar

6 large eggs

1 cup grated cotija or other salty white cheese

2 scallions, sliced

1 tablespoon chopped fresh parsley

crusty bread or baguette

1. Heat the olive oil in a large skillet over medium-high heat. Add the onion, garlic, and red pepper flakes and sauté until the onion begins to soften and take on some color, about 5 minutes.

2. Add the tomatoes, salt, sugar, and sherry vinegar and bring to a boil. Reduce the heat to bring the sauce to a low simmer and carefully crack in the eggs, making sure they are spaced evenly apart. Simmer, partially covered, until the egg whites are just cooked through but the yolks are still runny, about 7 minutes.

3. Remove from the heat and sprinkle with the cotija, scallions, and parsley. Serve with crusty bread to scoop up the sauce!

GRILLED CHEESE À LA PAULY CARMICHAEL

Paul Carmichael is the chef de cuisine at Má Pêche, the Momofuku outpost in Midtown Manhattan that also houses a Milk Bar. Many moons ago, when we were both cooks at wd~50, he made the most delicious grilled cheese sandwiches for family meal. I talked about them for years, though he swears there's nothing fancy about it at all.

While we were putting this book together, I finally convinced him to hand over his recipe so we could make them for ourselves. That's when we discovered the secret to his perfect grilled cheese: Kewpie mayonnaise. This realization confirmed what we already knew: Kewpie is the secret to any good recipe with mayonnaise as an ingredient. (Except for any recipe in this book that calls for Hellmann's mayonnaise, in which case, Hellmann's is the secret for *that* recipe. . . .) Kewpie is a Japanese mayonnaise with insane depth of flavor and umami notes.

8 teaspoons Kewpie mayonnaise
8 slices good sliced sandwich bread
8 teaspoons unsalted butter, at room temperature
8 slices American cheese

1. Spread 1 teaspoon of mayonnaise evenly over one side of each slice of bread and 1 teaspoon butter over the other side.

2. Top the butter side of 4 slices of bread with 2 slices of cheese each and then top that with the remaining slices of bread, mayonnaise side up. Butter on the inside, Kewpie mayonnaise on the outside—that's all you need to know.

3. Fry the sandwiches in lightly greased pans or a griddle over medium heat until golden brown and crispy, roughly 3 minutes per side. Eat while gooey and warm.

FRANNY'S RICE AND BEANS

— SERVES 4 TO 6 —

When Francisco Matos walked through our doors, Milk Bar life got a lot easier. He arrived with résumé in hand: He'd been a vet tech (we all bring our dogs to the offices above the kitchen), a fisherman (awesome), and a cook (perfect). He was rocking a long ponytail and a three-piece suit—HIRED! He quickly became our Renaissance man for all things big and small. There's a leak in the sink? Franny's got it. Someone ordered a hundred pallets of cookie mixes and they arrived on a truck without a lift gate? Franny's got that too.

　You know what else he's got? A badass recipe for family meal. Sometimes he makes it at home on his day off and surprises us with it the next day. Other times, he throws on a chef coat and makes it in the kitchen, right along with our cooks. This is a side dish that goes well with any simply cooked meat—in our kitchen, it's often a Bo Ssäm-style meat (see page 104). Long live Franny, and long live Franny-Meal!

1 tablespoon grapeseed or other neutral oil

½ pound kielbasa, cut into ¼-inch chunks

½ cup chopped white onion

1 teaspoon onion powder
½ teaspoon garlic powder
¼ teaspoon dried oregano
¼ teaspoon black pepper
1 tablespoon canned Goya sofrito

½ (15-ounce) can gandules (pigeon peas), rinsed and drained
1 cup long-grain white rice, rinsed and drained
1 tablespoon unsalted butter
1 (6.33-ounce) packet Goya Sazón
1 teaspoon kosher salt

1. Heat the oil in a large saucepan over medium-high heat. Add the kielbasa and sauté until browned, 2 to 3 minutes. Using a slotted spoon, remove the sausage from the pan, leaving the rendered fat in the pan.

2. Add the onion to the pan and cook over medium heat, scraping the bottom of the pan to dislodge the flavor-packed brown bits that are clinging to it, until the onion is translucent, 5 minutes.

3. Dump in the onion powder, garlic powder, oregano, pepper, and sofrito and let it caramelize for a minute. At this point, the mixture will look like a paste. Add the peas, rice, butter, sazón, kielbasa, and salt, then add enough water (about 4 cups) so everything is covered by 1 inch and give the mixture a few big stirs to make sure everything is incorporated. Bring the water to a boil and boil until the water has evaporated to the same level as the rice, about 5 minutes.

4. Reduce the heat to low, cover the pan tightly, and simmer for 25 to 30 minutes, until the rice is tender. Let rest off the heat for 10 minutes, then fluff with a fork and serve. It's FRAN-TASTIC!

BO SSÄM CHALLENGE

Sometimes even the hardest of bodies gets weeded in massive prep lists and too many things to do at once. When that's the case and 1 p.m. rears its ugly head, we fall back on our supply of bo ssäm–style pork. We almost always have it in-house because we use it in our pork buns, and with some rice or bread and a squirt bottle of whatever condiment you like (hoisin? Sriracha?), it makes a meal. (If you don't know, this style of bo ssäm is the creation of David Chang, the chef and chief heart-throb of the Momofuku restaurants. A big pork roast, it's the signature dish of Ssäm Bar and one of his most versatile creations.)

But why stop with pork, we ask?

The best thing about the technique David uses to cook the meat is that you can use it with any sizable cut of meat that's marbled or has a fat cap to keep it flavorful and moist while roasting in the oven. We call this the bo ssäm challenge—we dare you to find a protein that this recipe *doesn't* work for.

Don't know how to cook a hunk of beef, a goat shoulder, a saddle of lamb, a pork butt, or a skin-on turkey breast?! Coat it with this rub and slow-roast it—it will rise to the challenge.

Even if you're cooking for a small group or your nuclear family, go ahead and make a big-boy batch—there are plenty of recipes in this book that call for leftover slow-roasted meat: Party Nachos (page 207), Brisket and Broccoli (page 248), and more!

SERVES	2 TO 4	8 TO 10	15 TO 20
meat	a sensibly sized slab of something; about 3 pounds	a nice big marbled piece of meat; 8 to 10 pounds	a big boy: a whole pork shoulder or brisket, about 20 pounds
granulated sugar	1 cup	3 cups	6 cups
light brown sugar (packed)	2/3 cup	2 cups	4 cups
kosher salt	2/3 cup	2 cups	4 cups
black pepper	2 teaspoons	2 tablespoons	1/4 cup
time	3 to 4 hours, uncovered	6 to 8 hours, uncovered	10 to 12 hours, covered

SHRIMP BO SSÄM

You can also use this method to cook shrimp. Leave the shells on, toss them in some rub (about ½ cup for ½ pound of shellfish), and bake uncovered at 220°F for 30 to 40 minutes. Check them at 30 minutes: If they are opaque and pink-orange in hue, they're done; if not, put them back in the oven for up to 10 minutes more. They taste like classic Chinese salt-and-pepper shrimp!

GARLIC SHRIMP

For a flavor explosion akin to those had at the garlic shrimp shacks along the North Shore of Oahu, melt 1 tablespoon unsalted butter in a saucepan over high heat. Toss ½ pound shell-on shrimp with ½ cup rub and 3 tablespoons Caramelized Garlic (page 160), add to the pan, and cook for 5 minutes, or until the shrimp are opaque and pink-orange. Serve immediately over rice.

1. Heat the oven to 250°F.

2. Toss together the sugars, salt, and pepper in a large bowl.

3. Choose an appropriately sized roasting pan, baking dish, or oven-friendly pot. You want a dish that mimics the size of the meat you are cooking to ensure that the meat will cook drenched in its own juices as the fat begins to render in the oven. Put the meat into said baking receptacle.

4. Coat the protein, top, bottom, right, left—the entire surface area of the meat, including the fat or skin; don't miss a single spot, or you'll be sorry!—with the sugar mixture. Flip if necessary so the fat or skin is on top.

5. If cooking a huge cut, cover the roasting pan or pot with foil so it does not dry out over the course of the longer baking time. (If you are cooking a smaller cut of meat, it does not get covered.) Put the meat in the oven and consult the chart for the cooking time. For a large cut, which can take 10 to 12 hours, get it in the oven early in the morning—or just before bed! You'll know it's cooked through when the meat falls apart when prodded.

6. Let the meat cool slightly before serving or cutting up or shredding for other recipes.

BURNT-HONEY-BUTTER KALE WITH SESAME SEEDS

If you like crispy kale, or honey butter, or toasted sesame seeds, or all three, you will *love* this as your new healthy-unhealthy snack! It's also a great garnish on something fancier than a snack.

1 bunch (about ¾ pound) kale

2½ tablespoons Burnt-Honey Butter, melted and cooled slightly
2 teaspoons white sesame seeds
½ teaspoon kosher salt

1. Heat the oven to 200°F.

2. Remove and discard the stems from the kale. Slice the greens into 1-inch-wide strips.

3. Toss the kale with the melted honey butter, sesame seeds, and salt in a large bowl until evenly coated with the butter.

4. Spread the kale out on a baking sheet and bake for about 40 minutes, until it is fully dehydrated and crisp, like a paper-thin chip. Cool completely.

5. Store in an airtight container at room temperature for up to a week.

BURNT-HONEY BUTTER

MAKES ABOUT ¾ CUP

I love the flavor of burnt honey—sweet, bitter, a little savory from the salt I add—and use it in many iterations at Milk Bar. One of my favorites is making a burnt honey and butter mash-up for family-meal snacks. This is great on focaccia as well as kale, and it's superb eaten with a spoon straight out of the mixer. Make sure your gym membership is current so you can Jazzercise it off, because once you start eating it, you can't really stop.

¼ **cup** honey (nothing fancy)

8 **tablespoons (1 stick)** unsalted butter
½ **teaspoon** kosher salt

1. Heat the honey in a medium saucepan over medium heat until a candy thermometer registers 325°F, about 10 minutes. Make sure you use a decent-sized pan, because it will quadruple in volume while cooking—er, burning! The honey should go bubbly and deep brown like no place you've ever taken a pot of honey before. Please be careful, because hot honey can burn the living daylights out of you. And when you're checking the temperature of the honey, make sure the thermometer isn't touching the bottom of the pan, or you will get an inaccurately high reading.

2. Remove from the heat, add the butter and salt, and stir until the butter is completely melted. Cool completely, at room temperature or in the refrigerator, so the butter firms up.

3. Transfer the butter to the bowl of a stand mixer fitted with the paddle attachment and whip on high speed until it is lightened in color and completely smooth, with no chunks. Scrape down the sides of the bowl, crank the mixer back up to high speed, and whip for another 45 seconds, or until the butter is super-fluffy and light brown. Store in the refrigerator until ready to use or for up to 1 month.

I like blue cheese for its extra zing and funk, but cheddar will do fine too.

KIMCHI QUESADILLAS

Helen Jo, one of the very first Milk Bar employees, made this dish for family meal on the regs. It now ranks as the official Milk Bar throwback family meal of choice. Did we invent the kimchi quesadilla? Probably not; I think that was most likely our boy Roy Choi, of Kogi fame.

Start to finish, this snack takes about 15 minutes to throw together and the results are surprisingly good. I had my doubts the first time Helen made this, but after one bite, I floated away in kimchi quesadilla bliss and I haven't looked back since.

---

4 tablespoons (½ stick) unsalted butter, at room temperature

8 (6-inch) corn tortillas

1 cup kimchi (store-bought or homemade)

2 cups shredded or crumbled cheese (see note)
⅛ teaspoon black pepper

---

1. Heat the oven to 350°F.

2. Spread ½ tablespoon of the butter over each of 4 tortillas. Spread ¼ cup of the kimchi on top of each. Make it rain with ½ cup of the cheese and then a dusting of black pepper over each. Spread another ½ tablespoon butter on another 4 tortillas and place one on each stack, butter side down.

3. Put the quesadillas on a parchment-lined baking sheet, put another piece of parchment on top of the quesadillas, and top with another baking sheet. The weight and heat of the top pan in the oven ensures that the quesadillas fuse together in the baking process, and both sides are toasted in the process, no flip needed.

4. Bake for 7 minutes, or until the cheese has oozed out and caramelized the perimeters of the quesadillas. Remove the quesadillas from the oven and let them cool for a few minutes before devouring them. Slice if you like; we don't have time for that nonsense.

JERK CHICKEN

This is a special-occasion staple made by one of our most beloved cooks, Janee Humphreys. She no longer works at Milk Bar, but people still request her jerk chicken for their birthdays or going-away family meal, and she always stops by to bang out a batch, happily maintaining her family-meal-legend status. The dish, like its maker, is the perfect combination of salty, spicy, and sweet.

An aside to Janee: We miss you! Oh, and would you mind swinging by Milk Bar sometime next week to make us some jerk chicken? Thanks.

THE MARINADE

½ **cup** soy sauce

¼ **cup packed** light brown sugar

¼ **cup** grapeseed or other neutral oil

2 **tablespoons** honey

2 **teaspoons** kosher salt

2 **teaspoons** dried thyme

½ **teaspoon** ground allspice

½ **teaspoon** ground nutmeg

½ **teaspoon** ground cloves

1 **habanero**, seeds and all, roughly chopped

3 **scallions**, roughly chopped

2 **garlic cloves**, roughly chopped

1 **(1-inch) piece** fresh ginger, peeled, roughly chopped

4 **pounds** skin-on boneless chicken thighs

1. Make the marinade: Combine the soy sauce, brown sugar, oil, honey, salt, thyme, allspice, nutmeg, cloves, habanero, scallions, garlic, and ginger in a blender and blend until any large chunks are broken down.

2. Put the chicken in a large bowl, add the marinade, and use your hands to really work the marinade into the meat—this marinade is much drier than the Cookout/Bonfire ones and needs to be massaged into the chicken in order to penetrate it. (Don't forget to glove up or wash your paws in warm soapy water before and after this step.) Cover and refrigerate for at least 2, and up to 4, hours, tossing the chicken around every hour so it gets good and covered.

3. Heat the oven to 350°F.

4. Arrange the chicken on a wire rack set over a baking sheet. (This helps keep the bottoms from getting too wet, but it isn't absolutely necessary; you can arrange the chicken directly on a baking sheet if you don't have a rack.) Bake for 20 minutes, or until the jerk has blackened and no pink remains when you slice the meat.

Janee serves her jerk chicken with mango salsa, pineapple salsa, and coconut rice. Make your own salsas from scratch using your favorite recipes, or purchase from the grocery store.

BRISKET STROGANOFF

— SERVES 4 TO 6 —

This is a great way to use up leftover Bo Ssäm Challenge meat (see page 104). It doesn't have to be brisket—you can use whatever cut you like—but I like the way brisket tastes here best, so that's what's in the "official" recipe.

kosher salt

THE 'SHROOMS

½ **pound** button or cremini mushrooms, quartered

1 **tablespoon** unsalted butter, melted

1 **tablespoon** olive oil

2¼ **teaspoons** kosher salt

THE GRAVY

1 **tablespoon** unsalted butter

1 **medium** onion, diced

3 garlic cloves, diced

5 **tablespoons** Wondra flour

¼ **teaspoon** black pepper

2 **cups** beef stock

THE NOODS

1 **(12-ounce bag)** egg noodles

1 **tablespoon** unsalted butter

THE ASSEMBLY

¾ **cup** sour cream

2 **cups** cubed Bo Ssäm Challenge brisket (page 104)

1 **tablespoon** chopped fresh parsley

Wondra flour is a super-fine flour. It's great to use as the thickening agent in gravies and sauces because it doesn't lump as easily as regular all-purpose flour. A-P does make a fine substitute; it just won't incorporate as magically.

1. Heat the oven to 350°F.

2. Bring 5 quarts water to a boil in a large pot and salt it like the Mediterranean.

3. Prep the 'shrooms: Toss the mushrooms with the butter, oil, and salt in a large baking dish. Roast until tender and brown, about 20 minutes.

4. Meanwhile, get the gravy going: Melt the butter in a large saucepan over medium heat. Add the onion and garlic and cook until the onion softens and begins to color, about 10 minutes. Add the Wondra and pepper and whisk to ensure that all clumps of flour are broken up, then cook over low heat for 1 minute to release the starch. Whisk in the beef stock, bring the mixture to a boil, and cook for about 5 minutes, until the gravy begins to thicken. Keep warm.

5. Cook the noodles: Boil the egg noodles in the boiling water for about 6 minutes (or a minute shy of however long their package says to cook them), until al dente. Drain the noodles, put them in your serving vessel (which, in an ideal world, you would have warmed up in the oven), and toss them with the butter until it's melted and they're coated.

6. Put it together: While the pasta is cooking, add the roasted mushrooms, sour cream, and brisket to the stock mixture, stir together, and simmer over low heat until the gravy has thickened, about 10 minutes.

7. Spoon the beef over the noodles and top with the chopped parsley. Serve immediately.

XXXL LADY SALAD

In the warm summer months, our kitchen reaches sauna-like conditions, which means the last thing you want to see is hot, heavy food. At such times, a brigade of some of our favorite pastry cooks makes an XXXL bowl of hearty wild-card salads.

Now, I know what you're thinking. Salads are great served as part of a meal, but they rarely have the satiating factor needed to stand on their own. I'm with you on that. But! This is not the case with the XXXL Lady Salad. The quinoa, feta, blueberries, almonds, and herbs are already a recipe for success, and when they're mixed with a bangin' vinaigrette and some peppery arugula, well, . . . ladies and gentlemen alike will leave the table stuffed to the gills.

THE QUINOA
1 cup red quinoa
1 teaspoon kosher salt

THE FETA
2 tablespoons honey
1 tablespoon olive oil
½ pound feta cheese
black pepper

THE ALMONDS
½ cup slivered almonds

THE VINAIGRETTE
2 tablespoons sherry vinegar
1 lemon, juiced
2 teaspoons honey
1 teaspoon Dijon mustard
½ teaspoon fish sauce
⅛ teaspoon kosher salt

¼ cup olive oil

THE FRESH STUFF
4 cups arugula
1 pint blueberries
2 scallions, thinly sliced
1 tablespoon chopped fresh dill
1 tablespoon chopped fresh parsley
1 tablespoon chopped fresh cilantro

1. Heat the oven to 375°F.

2. Make the quinoa: Bring the quinoa and 2 cups water to a boil in a medium saucepan. Drop the heat to low and simmer until the quinoa is tender and the water has evaporated, 15 to 20 minutes. Fluff the quinoa with a fork and then let it cool to room temperature.

3. While the quinoa is cooking, bake the feta: Whisk together the honey and olive oil in a medium bowl. Cut the block of feta into ½-inch cubes, add to the bowl, and toss to coat. Sprinkle a little black pepper over and toss once more.

4. Spread the feta cubes on a baking sheet and bake for 15 minutes, or just until the feta begins to caramelize and brown. Set aside to cool.

5. Meanwhile, spread the slivered almonds on a small baking sheet and pop them into the oven for 5 minutes, or until they're just toasted and brown. Set aside to cool.

6. Make the vinaigrette: Whisk together the vinegar, lemon juice, honey, mustard, fish sauce, and salt in a medium bowl. Ratchet up your whisking to vigorous and drizzle in the olive oil in a steady stream until the dressing is completely smooth and beautifully emulsified.

7. Assemble the salad: Toss the quinoa, feta, and almonds with the arugula, blueberries, scallions, dill, parsley, and cilantro in a large bowl. Drizzle the dressing on top and give it a big final toss.

WEAK NIGHTS

I know what the television tells you, because it tells it to me too: that chefs and other food people, when they're done with work, stop in at some wonderful exotic restaurant where the chef treats them specially, or retire to their amazing home, fire up the hearth, and whip together some kind of "simple" Tuscan meal that takes only an hour or so, if you don't include snipping fresh herbs out in the garden.

Guess what? Sometimes scenarios like that do happen! But waaaaaay more common in my world is that I eat some beef jerky in my truck on the way home, call that dinner, and only change out of my work clothes when I wake up, ready to go back and do it again.

Many of my meals happen too late at night, often after I've remembered that I didn't actually make time to eat that day (other than tasting new items for Milk Bar). And if I'm not stuffing take-out into my face by then, I rush home and throw together something fast and easy. The meal is pretty "weak" by foodie standards, but I think my go-tos are not only pretty damn clever, but also pretty damn good.

In this chapter, I'm really letting you into my very-late-night, most desperate food moments. If you have a chip on your shoulder of any kind (unless it's a Cool Ranch Dorito), you should stop reading here. These recipes are made up of only what you can scrounge up in the pantry, at the bodega, or at the gas station. They are easy and don't require any planning. At all. They are not healthy. At all. They are not fancy or avant-garde or anything. Do not serve them to someone you are trying to impress. But they will put hair on your chest and make it easy to plop into bed, fed.

Each one of these recipes feeds one. If you've got a partner in crime, double up as needed.

COOKIE-DOUGH COOKIE

— MAKES 1 COOKIE —

What, might you ask, is a cookie-dough cookie? It's a confection made in a very hot oven, so that it looks like a perfectly baked cookie on the outside, but on the inside you have a gooey, unbaked cookie dough center. My. Dream. Come. True. The weakest of weak nights requires a minimum of one cookie-dough cookie.

This is one of the first cookies I tried making for the OG Milk Bar East Village location, but it never made it to the menu because the Health Department doesn't condone serving somewhat raw cookie dough. Bummer! (It also didn't work from a food-service standpoint, since the cookie-dough cookie has to be kept and served cold.) But at home, you are your own boss.

My secret is to have frozen cookie dough rounds in my freezer at home—always. How the heck else do you think my apartment always smells like freshly baked cookies when anyone comes over? That lends itself to this very special weak-night treat when no one is around.

I love this recipe best when made with classic Chocolate Chip Cookie dough (page 53).

---

1 (2¾-ounce) scoop cookie dough, frozen

---

1. Heat the oven to 500°F.

2. Put the frozen dough round on a greased or lined baking sheet and bake just until the cookie begins to spread and the thinnest of golden brown skins forms on the surface, but before the bottom of the cookie begins to burn, 4 to 5 minutes. Remove from the oven and immediately refrigerate until cool and set, about 15 minutes.

3. Eat.

BROWN-BUTTER CINNAMON TOAST

— SERVES 1 —

The weakest of weak-night "meals" is probably a bowl of cereal. For those nights where you have just enough energy to actually make something, forgo the bowl of Cinnamon Toast Crunch and make straight-up cinnamon toast instead.

This was my classic after-school or midnight snack as a kid, and it has followed me into adulthood.

I know what you're thinking—why put a recipe for cinnamon toast in a cookbook? Doesn't everyone already know how to make it? Well, to that I say, what if there is one person out there who doesn't? That person needs help. You can *give* a man some cinnamon toast, and he'll have a late-night snack for the evening, or you can *teach* a man to make cinnamon toast, and he'll have a late-night snack for life. I choose the latter.

Also, this cinnamon toast is different because it uses brown butter instead of regular butter. So there.

---

2 tablespoons unsalted butter

2 slices white bread

1 tablespoon sugar
¼ teaspoon ground cinnamon
pinch of kosher salt

---

1. Heat the oven to 325°F.

2. Put the butter in a microwave-safe bowl, cover it with a microwave-safe saucer or plate, and pop it into the microwave on high for 5 to 6 minutes. The butter will melt and then start to pop and brown. Don't be scared! Flavor is happening. Let it get deep brown in color and super-nutty in aroma. You just made brown butter.

3. When the brown butter has cooled slightly, stir in the extra-browned bits from the bottom of the bowl, then brush the browned butter onto both sides of each slice of bread, making sure to cover them completely.

4. Mix together the sugar, cinnamon, and salt in a small bowl or ramekin. Sprinkle evenly on both sides of the slices of bread.

5. Transfer the slices to a greased or lined baking sheet and bake for 10 to 15 minutes, until the bread is crisped up and golden brown yet still a smidge soft in the center. Eat at once.

Snyder's mini pretzels are closest to my heart, and the fancier you get with the blue cheese, the better; I like Queen Anne Stilton or Bayley Hazen Blue.

BLUE CHEESE PRETZELS

We love dipping things into stuff at Milk Bar. This recipe is the by-product of one of our managers' habit of dipping pretzels into a bowl of crumbled blue cheese. The problem was that the blue cheese would always fall off the dang pretzels. Geniuses that we are, we realized that if we baked the blue cheese onto the pretzels, it would melt, then caramelize and fuse with them, resulting in perfectly crunchy pretzels coated in a thin layer of tangy blue cheese.

1 cup mini pretzels
½ cup crumbled blue cheese

1. Heat the oven to 325°F.

2. Spread the pretzels in an even layer on a small baking sheet. Sprinkle the blue cheese evenly over them and bake for 7 minutes. The pretzels will be squishy and unappealing when they first come out of the oven. Let them cool completely in order to reach their full late-night snack potential.

EGG SOUP

When I started sharing my ideas for this book, a girlfriend of mine—a talented and powerful NYC woman, one I figured was too fancy to really embrace true weak-night cooking—lit up and squealed all at once when I was describing some of the dishes I was planning to include.

Her: EEEK! Please tell me you're going to include egg soup!

Me: I have no clue what egg soup is.

Her: Egg soup is the meal Amanda, Chela, and I each eat when we get home late at night after a long shoot or day of meetings or a marathon workday. It's *our* weak-night meal.

And so that is how I learned that when the white of a five-minute egg is cut up and tossed around in a bowl of its own warm gooey yolk, it is called *huevos tibios* in Mexico. And egg soup by fancy ladies in New York. It is the perfect late-night accompaniment to toasty bread and *Seinfeld* reruns.

1 large egg

kosher salt

black pepper
1 slice country-style bread, or more if desired, toasted

You can cook six eggs as easily as you can cook one egg using this recipe, as long as you don't take forever to add the eggs to the boiling water.

1. Bring a smallish saucepan of water to a boil. Add the egg and boil for exactly 5 minutes. This is a precise time, so use the timer on your phone; don't guesstimate.

2. With a slotted spoon, fish the egg out of the boiling water and transfer to a bowl of ice water. Let it sit until cool enough to handle, about 5 minutes.

3. Carefully crack and then peel open the egg (the yolk will still be runny), and use a spoon to scoop the white and yolk into a bowl. Cut up the white with the spoon, sprinkle with some salt and pepper, and sop up that soupy yolk with the toast.

GRILLED HAM AND CHEESE CORN COOKIE

— MAKES 1 SANDWICH —

This is another one of those recipes that seems like it may be weird. I'm here to tell you that it isn't, so take a chance and make it. The sweetness of the cookie lends itself perfectly to the salty ham and sharp cheddar cheese. This is also a great excuse to eat dessert and dinner at the same time. When it's 11 p.m., you really don't have time for a two-course meal.

2 slices sharp cheddar cheese
2 Milk Bar corn cookies
4 thin slices ham

1. Put a slice of cheese on the flat side of each cookie.

2. Warm the cookies, cheese side up, in a large skillet over medium heat. Pile up the sliced ham in an empty part of the skillet. Cook until the cookies and ham begin to brown and caramelize and the cheese has melted, 2 to 3 minutes.

3. Assemble a "sandwich" of cookie-cheese-ham-cheese-cookie on a plate or a paper towel. Eat.

If you've got a copy of *Momofuku Milk Bar*, you've got the recipe for corn cookies. Or you can buy some from milkbarstore.com and have them shipped to your doorstep. If not, Ritz Cookies (page 59) or Salt-and-Pepper Cookies (page 70) do the trick too.

STEWED TOMATOES

— SERVES 1 —

My mother used to make this when I was growing up, whipping it up in a jiffy during her busy tax season. Her mother made it for her too. Weak nights run deep in my family.

The recipe tastes like a better, thicker, homemade version of Campbell's tomato soup. It's great on a cold winter night, and it pairs perfectly with Ritz Cookies (page 59) or the Grilled Ham and Cheese Corn Cookie (page 124), for a delightful play on the classic tomato soup and grilled cheese combo.

2 tablespoons unsalted butter
2 tablespoons all-purpose flour
2 tablespoons sugar

1 (14.5-ounce) can diced tomatoes, drained, juices reserved

1½ teaspoons kosher salt
⅛ teaspoon black pepper

THE TOAST
2 slices white bread
1 tablespoon unsalted butter

1. Melt the butter in a medium saucepan over medium heat. Whisk in the flour and sugar and cook, whisking, until a thick paste has formed, about 3 minutes. Whisk in the tomato juices (just the juice!) and heat the mixture until it has thickened and begun to bubble up, about 2 minutes.

2. Add the diced tomatoes, salt, and pepper and cook until heated through, about 3 minutes.

3. Meanwhile, toast and then butter the bread.

4. Cut the bread into 1-inch cubes and serve with the stewed tomatoes.

SPAGHETTIOS SAMMY

— MAKES 1 SANDWICH —

It's around midnight on a Wednesday. You just got home from work, and you skipped dinner to finish that margin index fluctuation report with your cubicle-mate Jerry. You're peckish as hell. The cupboard is bare, save a can of SpaghettiOs, some eggs, and a couple of other choice gems you typically keep on hand (potato chips and frozen breakfast sausage, for example). You'll eat anything at this point. Literally *anything,* even a sandwich made with SpaghettiOs . . .

1 large egg

1 (7.5-ounce) can SpaghettiOs

4 maple-flavored breakfast sausage links

2 slices bread, preferably potato bread
unsalted butter (optional)
maple syrup (optional)
handful of chips

1. Put the egg in a small microwave-safe bowl, cover it with water, and microwave for 2 minutes and 15 seconds. Remove the egg from the water and set it aside to cool while you make the rest of the sandwich; reserve the bowl of water.

2. Dump the can of SpaghettiOs into a microwave-safe bowl and microwave for 1 minute and 30 seconds, or until warm. Alternatively, heat in a small saucepan on the stove.

3. Cook the breakfast sausage in the microwave or in a skillet on the stove until warm and crispy on the outside.

4. Gently crack the egg and peel it, submerged in the water it was microwaved in. It's much easier this way.

5. Assemble the sandwich: You can really do this however you want—at this point does it even matter?—but here is how I do it: Lay the sausage links on one slice of bread, toasted and buttered for extra credit points, with a drizzle of maple syrup if you need more maple vibes, or are worried it won't be sweet enough for you. Add the warm SpaghettiOs on top, throw on a handful of chips for crunch, and top with the soft egg. Crown it with the remaining piece of potato bread, toasted and buttered, if you like. Press down until the egg pops open and the yolky goodness oozes over the whole mess (see page 116). Eat immediately.

This infamous sandwich has been known to steal hearts on first dates too.

Every microwave is different. The difference between a perfectly cooked egg and an egg explosion is a matter of seconds, so be careful and test it out a few times to find the timing that works best for you. If you don't have a microwave, soft-boil the egg à la Egg Soup (see page 122).

For the chips, sour cream and onion potato chips are good. So are Doritos.

BIRD IN A BAG

— SERVES 1 —

Staring over from the pastry station as I prepped petits fours nightly, I used to see the savory chefs at Bouley make a very fancy version of this bird. One dinner service I figured, why not just bootleg the technique for my late-night post-work snack?

This is Milk Bar's version of Modernist cuisine. We call it Modernish Milk Bar. It's my quickie take on sous-vide cooking and it's a fun way to cook that is also really cool. Like, really, really cool.

1 boneless, skinless chicken breast half or thigh

1 teaspoon seasoning, such as the seasoning mixes for Milk Bar Ranch Dip (page 175) or the Chorizo Burgers (page 178), or the always classic salt and pepper

1 cup buttermilk

1. Put a quart-sized zip-top freezer bag in a small bowl, leaving the mouth of the bag gaping open. (This is the best way to get all of the ingredients inside the bag without making a mess!) Evenly coat the chicken with seasoning and put it in the bag. Pour in the buttermilk.

2. Seal the bag tightly, making sure there is little-to-no air left in it. A trick to getting air out of a freezer bag is to seal it almost all the way, with just enough space to slip a straw in, then use the straw to suck the air out (be careful not to suck up any of the milk inside the bag—gross!) and seal immediately. Put the bag inside a gallon-size plastic freezer bag. Seal that one just as tightly as you sealed the first one, but leave a little bit of air in it. This double bagging is insurance against one of the bags accidentally coming open in the cooking process.

3. Fill a medium saucepan three-quarters full with water and bring the water to a low simmer. Add a trivet or aluminum foil shaped into a doughnut to the water to ensure that the chicken won't come in contact with the bottom of the pan. Add the bag o' chicken and poach for 12 to 15 minutes, until the chicken is just cooked through, depending on its size and thickness.

4. Remove the bag from the water, carefully open it up (beware of steam burns), and remove the chicken. The heat-treated buttermilk is now garbage—it gets funky and separates when heated this way. Just dump it; it has already done its work. Dig in.

If the chicken breast is very large, slice it in half lengthwise (i.e., butterfly or fillet it) before cooking.

For one of my healthier weaknight meal faves, I serve the chicken with Burnt-Honey-Butter Kale (page 106).

TANG TOAST

Did you know Dutch folk eat toasted white bread with butter and sprinkles? Grown-ups eat it on the regular, and *no one* flinches!

If you can't quite channel your inner Netherlander, and cinnamon and sugar ain't your steez, maybe Tang toast is!

This odd combo is big in the Christian church community that I was exposed to growing up in central Ohio. Think about it: what's the only thing left in church kitchens Monday through Saturday? Some white bread, tainted margarine, and the remnants of some Tang. This recipe is perfect both for churches running low on supplies and for late nights when you're running low on energy.

---

2 slices white bread
1 tablespoon margarine (not butter)
½ teaspoon Tang drink mix

---

1. Toast the bread.

2. Slather each slice of toast with margarine, add a sprinkle of Tang to each one, and eat.

DESPERATION NACHOS

— SERVES 1 —

The only rule for desperation nachos is that there are no rules. These have the look and feel of the classic party nachos on page 207 but are *far* more janky. Use your imagination—and, more important, whatever's left in your pantry and refrigerator—to come up with these "nachos." The funkier the better. Don't be afraid to get, *ahem* . . . creative.

You will need at least one item from each category.

"CRACKERS": stale chips, Doritos, crackers, wafers, Fritos, anything crispy and crunchy. This will be the vehicle that transfers the other ingredients to your mouth.

"CHEESE": Cheez Whiz, queso (as in liquid melted cheese—or cheese dip, if you will), cheddar, Manchego, or a combination of all the cheeses left in your cheese drawer that are too small to use for any other purpose. This will be the melty, gooey part that fuses all the other ingredients to the "cracker."

"VEGETABLE": capers, olives, jalapeños, beans and taco sauce, zucchini, canned tomatoes (fine, they're a fruit), any vegetables you have lying around that need to be used up, or even dried oregano (a little sprinkle will do you). This is the "fresh" part of the recipe.

"MEAT": cream of chicken soup, liquid drained off; sandwich meat torn into small pieces; bacon bits; chicken nuggets; leftover Bo Ssäm Challenge meat (page 104); breakfast sausage crumbles; can o' Hungry Man. Whatever you have that you like will work great.

"SAUCE": This one's optional, but if you're lucky, you have a quarter of a jar of salsa, a tub of sour cream, some Milk Bar Ranch Dip (page 175), or another dip-like item at the back of your fridge that you can dunk each bite into.

---

1. Heat the oven to 350°F.

2. Spread a thin, even layer of "crackers" on a baking sheet. Top with the "cheese." Top the "cheese" with the "vegetable." Throw some "meat" on all of this for good measure.

3. Put the nachos in the oven and bake until the cheese has melted (if it's the kind of cheese that melts) or until the ingredients have warmed to your liking and palate. Dip into "sauce," if applicable.

These aren't supposed to be gastronomic mind-blowing delicacies. They are solely for sustenance.

If you don't have enough fixins in your cupboards to make the most desperate of desperation nachos, a variation on this recipe is Bodega Nachos, wherein you run to the closest convenience store and gather any items that might seem fit to make up a plate of nachos. You have slightly more choice, so the nachos are inevitably seasoned with less despair, but delicious nonetheless.

PICKLE-JUICE-POACHED FISH

— SERVES 1 —

One of my favorite food moments of 2013 was eating pickle-juice-poached fish at Tasty China II, Peter Chang's restaurant just outside of Atlanta, with two of my favorite culinary personalities, Danny Bowien and Chris Ying. Apparently this is an OG Szechuan cooking technique, and I, of course, was head over heels for it, knowing that it would quickly become weak-night worthy. The flavor of the pickle juice allows you to get away without any additional seasoning—so genius!

Juice from 2 (16-ounce) jars pickle spears, the more radioactive green, the better

1 teaspoon sugar

1 (6- to 8-ounce) fresh white fish fillet (I love cod or halibut)

1. Pour the pickle juice and sugar into a sauté pan small enough that the juice comes about ¼ inch up the sides. Heat the juice over medium heat until it boils, then reduce the heat so the liquid simmers and stir to dissolve the sugar. Add the fish fillet and poach, uncovered, for 2 minutes. Gently flip and continue poaching until cooked through and opaque, 1 to 2 minutes, depending on the thickness of the fillet.

2. Remove the fillet from the pan and put in a bowl. Bring the pickle liquid back to a boil and boil until reduced by more than half; you're depending on the sweet, salty zing and aromatics to be the final seasoning agent, so let it thicken slightly. Pour the liquid over the fish and enjoy.

Chop up one of the pickles from the jar and sprinkle on top of the fish for extra zing.

It may be a weak night tonight, but maybe you're planning for a cookout sometime soon? Pickle juice also makes a great chicken wing marinade (see page 192).

FREAKIN' WEEKEND

On the rare weekend I have off, R. Kelly's "Ignition (Remix)" plays on repeat in my head as I pantomime driving a tricked-out buggy rather than the pickup truck I actually own.

When I was a kid, we spent our weekends running errands and taking care of others, not cooking a big ol' meal at home, so I've reveled in the act of starting my own freakin' tradition to celebrate a proper day off. Nothing seems more romantic to me than pouring a glass of wine, roasting a chicken, and being calm. Except that's not exactly how a freakin' weekend goes down in my house. I can't sit still, so I pop out of bed early, not wanting to miss a moment of freedom. I sip a cup of coffee, whip up some cake batter to throw in a Crock-Pot, and then dive into the poultry recipe to cook a savory feast.

My brain, crazy as it is, loves knowing there's no way in hell I'm going to eat a whole roasted chicken, so my gears immediately start turning, imagining how I'm going to cook up all kinds of chicken dishes with the leftovers to feed myself and others in the days that follow.

I also like to spend the time the chicken is in the oven in a calm-but-buzzing state of making big-batch staples. These are things I'll use to spruce up weak-night creations or chicken-day leftovers; in my experience, a batch of soft-poached eggs or caramelized leeks never goes to waste over the course of a week. Nor does a jar of miso butterscotch.

As such, my freakin' weekend is all about one day of heavy-duty cooking that results in a really delicious (yet still simple and family-friendly) dinner that also produces enough left-overs to be cleverly and efficiently recombined into meals to feed me, and anyone else joining in, for the bustling week ahead!

CROCK-POT CAKE

Mix this batter in the morning and throw it into the Crock-Pot so its warm goo will await you after dinner. Alternatively, mix the batter at night, throw it into the Crock-Pot, and sleep tight, knowing you'll have a warm cake waiting for you when you wake up. Either way, you've got it made in the shade.

½ **pound (2 sticks)** unsalted butter, at room temperature
1¼ **cups** granulated sugar
¼ **cup packed** light brown sugar

3 large eggs
1½ **teaspoons** vanilla extract

¾ **cup** buttermilk
⅓ **cup** grapeseed or other neutral oil

1½ **cups** cake flour
1 teaspoon baking powder
1 teaspoon kosher salt

1. Combine the butter and both sugars and cream on medium-high in the bowl of a stand mixer fitted with the paddle attachment until fluffy and pale, 2 to 3 minutes. Mix in the eggs and vanilla, then paddle the mixture on medium-high for 3 minutes, or until it's homogenous and fluffy. Add the buttermilk and oil.

2. On very low speed, add the cake flour, baking powder, and salt, mixing for 45 to 60 seconds, just until the batter comes together. Scrape down the sides of the bowl. If you spot any lumps of cake flour, mix for another 45 seconds.

3. Pour the batter into a greased Crock-Pot. Depending on the age and strength of your appliance, cook on low for 4 to 6 hours, until the cake has set and is fully cooked through in the center.

4. Spoon the cake directly from the pot onto plates. Eat warm.

DAY 1 ROAST CHICKEN...

— SERVES 2 TO 4, WITH LEFTOVERS —

It doesn't take much to roast a chicken right, but everyone does it differently. I like to leave my bird covered nearly the entire time (this method keeps the juice and flavor in the bird; read more on this dorky mentality in Magnus Nilsson's *Fäviken* cookbook), then blast the gal on broil at the very end for a crisp skin moment.

1 (4- to 5-pound) whole chicken, gizzards removed

1 lemon, sliced lengthwise and then into half-moons, seeded
12 fresh thyme sprigs
6 to 10 garlic cloves (to taste), smashed and peeled
4 tablespoons (½ stick) unsalted butter, at room temperature or partly melted

2 tablespoons kosher salt
1 teaspoon black pepper

1. Position an oven rack so that the top of the chicken will be centered in the oven (i.e., not too close to the top). Heat the oven to 375°F.

2. Stuff the area between the skin and each breast and each leg with 1 lemon slice, 1 thyme sprig, and 1 smashed garlic clove. Stuff its cavity with the remaining lemon, thyme, and garlic. Rub the top of the skin down with some of the soft butter, like it's sunscreen going on a toddler; stuff the remaining butter inside the cavity with the aromatics. Sprinkle the salt and pepper over all. Put the chicken breast side up in a deep baking dish or a Dutch oven.

3. Roast the chicken, covered with a lid, for 50 to 60 minutes, until the juices run clear when you make a small cut between the thigh and leg. (If for some reason you choose not to cover the bird, your roast time will increase by 15 to 20 minutes, as it will take longer for the heat to penetrate the center.)

4. Remove the lid, and broil the chicken on high, keeping an overbearingly close eye on it, until the skin crisps up nicely and is golden brown, about 5 minutes.

5. Carve and serve your bird. I only make Overnight Chicken Soup (page 152) with any leftovers—it's easy cleanup and leaves no piece of the bird behind. But if you're planning a picnic the next day, I'd be OK if you picked a cup or two of meat to stash in the fridge for chicken salad (use the recipe for Smoked Turkey Salad, page 184; just cut it in half).

(recipe continues)

The quality of the chicken really does make a difference. Find the one that works best for you. I love a 5-pound Bell & Evans chicken to serve me and three gal pals, or me and a hunky man, with leftovers.

If you're looking to feed a larger crowd, entertain the notion that you may want several smaller birds rather than a bigger chick, which will probably have less flavor and take far longer to roast.

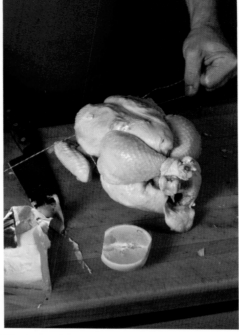

I rarely tie up my birds because I can usually find only embroidery thread at home. Feel free to truss 'em if you've got the twine.

...WITH VEGETABLES

While the chicken is roasting, you can use the time—and oven heat, if you'd like—to make some, gasp, vegetables.

ROASTED VEG

Clean out your fridge and cut any old/renegade vegetables into 1-inch wedges. Toss them with salt and pepper and add them to the chicken 20 to 30 minutes before it's done. There will be plenty of rendered drippings in there to infuse them with a ton of flavor, and the bird will pick up some additional veg notes too.

ROASTED OKRA

Keep okra whole or cut it into ½-inch pieces, toss with oil to coat, and season with salt and paprika. Spread evenly on a baking sheet and roast on an oven rack underneath the chicken for 15 minutes, or until lightly caramelized and tender. Note that this is best in early and main okra season. At the tail end of the season, the veg gets very woody and can make this preparation hit-or-miss.

CORN ON THE COB

The money move in the summer is to shuck and roast or boil corn on the cob before rolling it in the pan drippings from the roast chicken to season just before eating.

BLACK-PEPPER-BUTTER MASHED POTATOES

— SERVES 4 —

The secret to these delicious mashed potatoes, obviously, is sugar.

2 pounds potatoes, washed and cut into 1-inch pieces

8 tablespoons (1 stick) unsalted butter, at room temperature
2 tablespoons whole milk
1 tablespoon sugar
2 teaspoons kosher salt
1 teaspoon black pepper

1. Fill a large pot with cold water, add the potatoes, bring to a boil over high heat, and boil until fork-tender, about 15 minutes.

2. Drain the potatoes and transfer to a bowl. Add the butter, milk, sugar, salt, and pepper and mash by hand. Serve hot.

For super-smooth potatoes, use a stand mixer fitted with the paddle attachment. Mix on medium until mashed together, about 2 minutes. Then mix on high just until light and fluffy, about 1 minute (longer will make black pepper–mashed potato glue, so be mindful of the time).

CASSEROLE

Leftover mashed potatoes make a bang-up casserole when mixed with a little sour cream, spooned into a greased baking dish, and baked alone or with leftover cooked veggies or meat scraps on top at 350°F for 45 minutes.

ONE-BOWL DINNER ROLLS

— MAKES 1 DOZEN ROLLS

Nothing speaks to my heart like a warm, soft dinner roll, made fresh. You have plenty of time while your chicken is roasting to whip up a batch of these. And all it takes is one bowl . . .

3 cups all-purpose flour, plus more for dusting

¼ cup sugar

2 teaspoons kosher salt

1 (¼-ounce) package active dry yeast

¾ cup very hot water

⅓ cup canola oil, plus more for the bowl and brushing

1 large egg

1. Combine the flour, sugar, salt, and yeast in the bowl of a stand mixer fitted with the dough hook, add the hot water and oil, and mix on low speed to just combine. Add the egg and mix for 7 minutes, or until smooth and well kneaded.

2. Remove the bowl from the mixer and move the dough around in the bowl so you can grease the sides lightly with about 1 teaspoon oil. Let the dough rise, covered, for 1 hour in a quiet, draft-free place (I put mine in the microwave or oven, turned off), or until doubled in size.

3. Grease a 9 × 12-inch baking dish or two smaller pans, such as Bundt pans.

4. Punch the dough down, turn it out onto a floured countertop, and divide it into 12 equal pieces. Roll each one into a ball and arrange seam side down and ½ inch apart from each other in the prepared baking dish. Let rise again, covered, until doubled in size, 1 hour.

5. Heat the oven to 350°F. Gently coat the tops of the proofed rolls with 2 teaspoons oil. (Use a pastry brush or, like R. Kelly would, your fingers.) Bake for 10 to 15 minutes, until the tops are golden brown. Brush the roll tops with oil again after they come out of the oven, and serve!

KITCHEN-SINK QUICHE

— SERVES 6 TO 8 —

While the chicken is roasting, I like to make a quiche for the next morning—it's a real Freakin' Weekend treat! I tuck it into the oven once I take my bird out, to bake while I eat dinner.

THE CRUST

1½ **cups** all-purpose flour, plus more for rolling

2 **tablespoons** sugar

¾ **teaspoon** kosher salt

8 **tablespoons (1 stick)** unsalted butter, very soft

1½ **tablespoons** cold water

THE FILLING

½ **pound** sliced sandwich meat, such as ham or turkey

6 **large** eggs

½ **cup** whole milk

¼ **cup** sour cream

2 **teaspoons** kosher salt

½ **teaspoon** black pepper

1 **cup** shredded cheese, such as cheddar

¼ **cup** Sweet-and-Sour Red Onion Jam (page 215)

¼ **cup** Caramelized Onions (page 159)

1. Prepare the crust: Combine the flour, sugar, and salt in the bowl of a stand mixer fitted with the paddle attachment. Add the butter and mix until it is in pea-sized pieces and well distributed. With the mixer on low, add the cold water, mixing just until the dough begins to come together.

2. Dump the dough out of the bowl, then gently clump it together with your hands to form a 1-inch-thick patty. Wrap in plastic wrap and put it in the refrigerator to rest and chill for 30 minutes.

3. While the dough is chilling, prep the filling: Start by griddling the sandwich meat in a hot skillet or pan until browned. Let cool, then chop.

4. Heat the oven to 375°F.

5. Crack the eggs into a large bowl and whisk in the milk, sour cream, salt, and pepper. Stir in the cheese, both kinds of onions, and the sandwich meat.

6. Take the dough out of the fridge and, on a lightly floured work surface, roll it into a 12-inch circle. Put a 10-inch pie dish upside down on the dough and flip the two over. Using your fingertips, gently press the dough into the pan, then crimp the crust around the edges.

7. Pour the filling into the crust. Bake for 30 to 45 minutes, until the eggy center is just set. Keep a close watch! For a perfect top, broil for a minute or two at the very end of the baking process.

DAYS 1+2 OVERNIGHT CHICKEN SOUP

— SERVES 4 TO 6 —

Roast chicken leftovers + water = baller chicken soup, and one of my favorite things to cook, because it makes my entire apartment smell legit the next morning, and I've barely done a thing.

  I can never consume enough chicken at one dinner to be done with the bird there. So I look to the childhood kitchen lessons I learned from my grandmother. I use EVERY. LAST. BIT. of meat and carcass to make something equally delicious.

roast chicken carcass with some meat attached (on the wings, back, etc.) and any leftover aromatics (garlic, herbs, etc.)

¼ to ½ cup soy sauce (I like Kikkoman)
⅓ to ⅔ cup apple cider or apple juice
¼ to ½ teaspoon black pepper

1. While you're doing the dishes, combine the chicken carcass and any residual meat and leftover aromatics in a large stockpot (5- to 8-quart capacity) and fill the pot with water so the chicken is fully submerged. Set over the lowest of low heat, lid that puppy three-quarters of the way so the water can evaporate a little bit but not too much, and leave it overnight.

2. Wake up. Your kitchen smells amazing, right? Strain the liquid from the chicken into another large pot. Brush your teeth. Brush your hair. The chicken should be cool enough to handle at this point.

3. Separate all chicken meat from the bones, aromatics, and gelatin. Don't be grossed out—put your best farm girl face on, roll up your sleeves, and get to work. This should yield 2 to 3 cups light and dark meat, depending on how much chicken you ate the night before. Compost the bones and stuff.

4. You will now see two layers in the pot of chicken liquid. The top layer is a yellow oil slick of chicken fat and the chicken broth is below it. With a large spoon, skim off ¼ cup chicken fat and refrigerate to use for Chicken Fat Biscuits (page 154). Add the pulled chicken to the pot with the remaining fat and broth and refrigerate until dinnertime.

5. When the clock strikes dinner, take the pot out of the fridge and bring the soup to a simmer over medium heat. Season with soy sauce, apple cider, and black pepper to taste.

Clean out your fridge when the soup is almost ready by throwing in a handful of baby carrots, chopped onion, Brussels sprouts, or spinach. Whatever you've got will taste awesome in a veggie-fortified chicken soup.

If you like rice or pasta, cook some up in a separate pot, stealing some broth from the soup pot to use as your cooking liquid.

EGG DROP CHICKEN SOUP

Whisk up 3 eggs. In a slow, steady stream, pour into the finished soup, stirring the egg stream rapidly in a clockwise direction for 1 to 2 minutes, until ribbons form. Garnish with thinly sliced scallions, if you've got 'em.

I *know*. Why must I always ask you to break the rules? It drives my family crazy when I make this in their kitchen and demand to leave an open flame a-burnin' overnight. But this is the way I do it! This process steeps every last slurp of flavor into the soup: The depth is insane when you roll slow and low, challenging reason and basic safety, leaving a whole carcass, with plenty of meat on it, to simmer overnight. The meat remains incredibly tender, it's much easier to pick every last shred, *and* you don't have to deal with any prep work post-dinner—just cover the bird with water and say, "Night, night."

CHICKEN FAT BISCUITS

— MAKES ABOUT 1 DOZEN BISCUITS —

If, for some strange reason, you did not follow me on the chicken fat train, any animal fat, such as lard or unsalted butter, will do in these tender biscuits. This dough is also used to make the dumplings in the recipe on the next page.

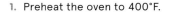

2 cups all-purpose flour
1 teaspoon sugar
½ **teaspoon** kosher salt
1 teaspoon baking powder
¼ **teaspoon** baking soda

¼ **cup** cold rendered chicken fat (reserved from
   making Overnight Chicken Soup, page 152), plus
   more for brushing if desired

¾ **cup** buttermilk (or a scant ¾ cup whole milk plus
   a splash of vinegar)

1. Preheat the oven to 400°F.

2. Combine the flour, sugar, salt, baking powder, and baking soda in a large bowl. Squish the chicken fat into the dry ingredients by rubbing it between your fingertips until the fat is in pea-sized pieces and well distributed. Add the buttermilk and mix together until a shaggy dough forms.

3. Dump out the contents of the bowl onto a countertop and knead 5 to 8 times, until the dough is a solid mass. The more you touch and work the dough, the less light and awesome your biscuits will be.

4. Gently flatten the dough into a 1-inch-thick slab. Using a knife or sharp square cutter, cut the dough into 2-inch squares. (Throw away dull cutters! They will compress the dough and make less fluffy biscuits.) Transfer to a greased or lined baking sheet, 2 inches apart.

5. Bake the biscuits for 7 to 8 minutes, until golden brown. Brush a little extra chicken fat on top if you want those biscuits shiny. Eat warm out of the oven!

CHICKEN AND DUMPLINGS

— SERVES 2 TO 4 ————————————

When I tire of living on chicken soup, I take some soup and make it into chicken and dumplings.

3 cups veggie-fortified Overnight Chicken Soup (see page 152)

½ recipe Chicken Fat Biscuits dough (opposite), prepared through step 3

1. Pour the chicken soup into a medium pot and bring to a simmer over medium heat.

2. Flatten the biscuit dough into a ½-inch slab and cut into 1-inch squares. Arrange in an even layer on top of the simmering soup. With a large spoon or ladle, spoon hot broth over the top of the biscuit dough as it cooks for 3 to 4 minutes, or until the dumplings float and are no longer doughy. Spoon into bowls and serve.

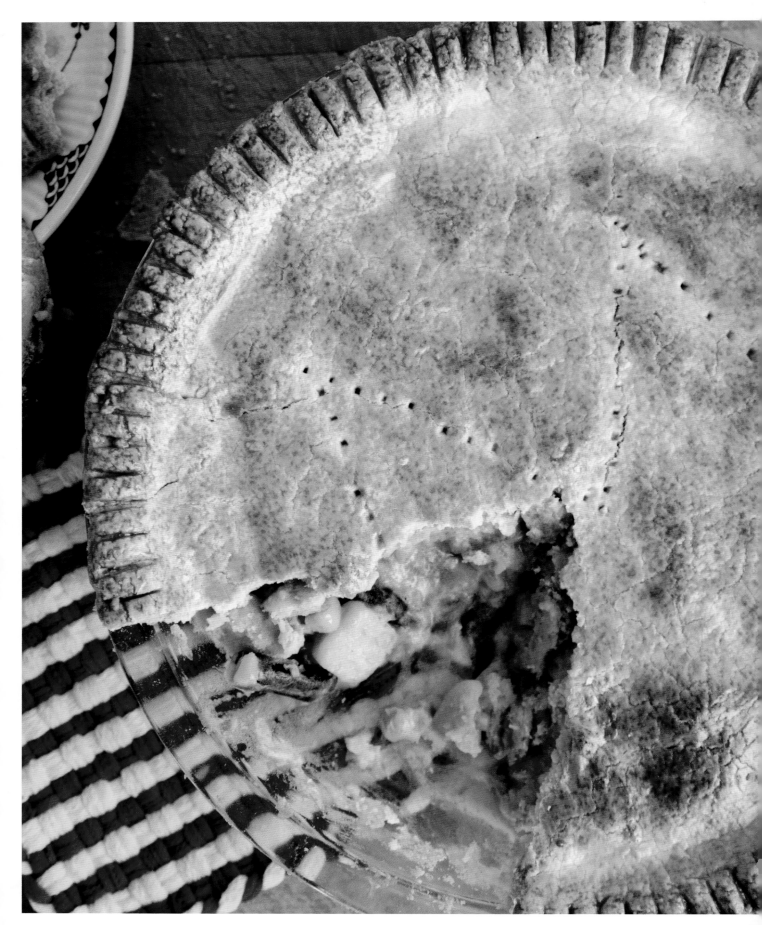

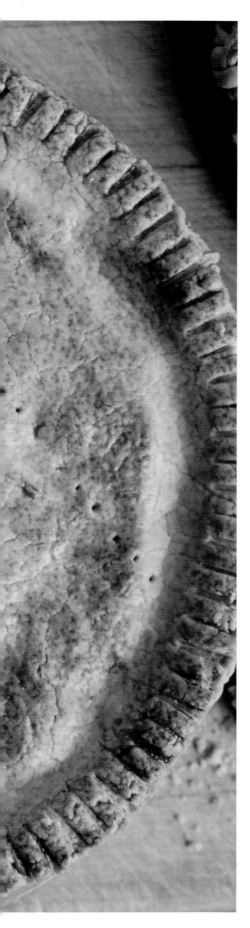

CHICKEN POTPIE

— SERVES 2 TO 4 —

If I want to revive my chicken soup with the use of a flaky pie crust rather than pillowy poached dumplings (see page 155), I make chicken potpie. Eat your heart out, Marie Callender!

---

3 cups veggie-fortified Overnight Chicken Soup (see page 152)
1 teaspoon Wondra flour

1 recipe Kitchen-Sink Quiche crust (page 151), chilled

1 large egg
½ teaspoon water

---

1. Heat the oven to 325°F.

2. Heat 1 cup of the chicken soup in a medium saucepan over medium heat until it boils. Whisk in the Wondra and heat the soup until warm to the touch and viscous. (This is just to thicken the soup.) Stir in the remaining 2 cups cold soup to cool the mixture down quickly and easily.

3. Grab four oven-friendly bowls or ramekins; a 9-inch glass or ceramic pie dish will do too. Divide the thickened chicken mixture evenly among the bowls, or pour it into the pie dish.

4. Take the dough out of the fridge. If using individual bowls, divide the dough into 4 equal pieces. On a lightly floured work surface, roll it into 4 rounds, each 1 inch larger in diameter than the mouth of the bowls. Or roll the whole piece of dough into a 10-inch circle. Put the dough atop the bowls or pie dish and, using your fingertips, gently press the dough around the edges to seal and crimp the crust.

5. Whisk together the egg and water in a small bowl with a fork. Brush the egg wash over the dough and, with a fork or sharp knife, make pinpoint insertions into each top in the shape of yours or your guest's initials.

6. Bake the potpies until the crust is golden brown and the filling is beginning to bubble out of the initialed top, 30 minutes for bowls and 45 for a pie dish. Carefully remove from the oven and let cool for 10 minutes before serving. You don't want to burn the roof of your mouth!

POACHED EGGS

— ADAPTED FROM *MOMOFUKU* | MAKES AS MANY AS YOU'D LIKE —

I put poached eggs on *everything,* from the obvious Eggs Benedict (page 232) to leftover fried rice from my Chinese-food splurge the night before. A soft pillowy white with warm runny yolk makes everything taste brand-new. This slow-poaching method is foolproof for poaching a lot of eggs at once.

large eggs

1. Fill your biggest, deepest pot with water and put it on the stove over the lowest possible heat. Use something to keep the eggs from sitting on the bottom of the pot: a cake rack or a steamer rack is ideal. A doughnut of aluminum foil will also work.

2. Use an instant-read thermometer to monitor the temperature of the pot—it should be between 140° and 145°F; if it's too hot, add cold water or an ice cube. Add the eggs to the pot and let them bathe for 40 to 45 minutes, checking the temperature regularly with the thermometer or by sticking your finger in the water (it should be the temperature of a very hot bath) and moderating it as needed.

3. You can use the eggs immediately or submerge them in an ice bath to cool before storing them in the refrigerator for up to 1 week. Warm the eggs under piping-hot tap water for 1 minute before serving.

4. To serve, crack the eggs one at a time into a small saucer. Tip the dish to pour off the loosest part of the white, then slide the egg onto the dish it's destined for.

CARAMELIZED ONIONS

— ADAPTED FROM *MOMOFUKU* | MAKES ABOUT 1 CUP —

My all-time favorite vegetable is the onion, mostly because it lends a complex sweetness to any savory dish. My heart of hearts lives in the caramelized onion. I love that you cannot rush the process and I love even more that it brings great depth to any dish with its creamy, sweet, and caramel notes. I use caramelized onions every place I can—breakfast, lunch, and dinner. They go in makeshift morning hash browns, on any nacho extravaganza I assemble on the fly, and atop any leafy green salad come dinner. As such, you can always find a supply of caramelized onions on my person, or at the very least in my fridge, at all times.

2 tablespoons grapeseed or other neutral oil

6 medium Spanish onions, thinly sliced

2 teaspoons kosher salt

1. Heat the oil in a large sauté pan over medium-high heat for 1 to 1½ minutes, until it's very, very hot but not smoking. Add the onions to the pan—they will be piled high, probably to the rim—and let them cook undisturbed for 2 to 3 minutes.

2. Carefully toss the onions and get comfy—you have 50 minutes of onion cookery ahead of you. Here's what you're looking for:

   a. For the first 15 minutes or so, the onions on the bottom of the pan should slowly but steadily take on color as they sweat out their liquid. Do not press down on them with a spatula or jack up the heat to try to accelerate this process, but do turn the whole pile over on itself every 3 to 4 minutes.

   b. After the mass of onions has significantly reduced in volume—the onions will be softer and more supple and have fallen considerably—turn the heat to medium-low and stir the onions every 10 minutes or so, making sure they don't stick or burn. This is the part that matters: the onions should get soft and sweet but not dried out.

   c. After 50 minutes or so, the onions should have shrunk considerably and have a definite sweetness, a deep roasted flavor, and a texture that's just this side of mushy. Season them with salt and use them right away, or let cool and then store in the refrigerator, tightly covered, for up to a week.

CARAMELIZED GARLIC

— MAKES ABOUT 1 CUP —

Though I don't personally partake in all the vampire mania out there, I eat enough garlic on a regular basis to fight off any bad guys.

I fell in love with what caramelized, nearly burnt garlic can do for you on the North Shore of Oahu, jumping from garlic-shrimp shack to garlic-shrimp shack (see page 105 for a simple rendition). Now I eat it by the spoonful, or throw it on top of a pizza (see page 235), tuck it into a late-night sandwich, or add it to anything I might be cooking up when cleaning out the fridge.

4 tablespoons (½ stick) unsalted butter

5 heads garlic, separated into cloves, smashed, peeled, and chopped

1 teaspoon kosher salt

1. Melt the butter in a large sauté pan over *very* low heat. Add the garlic, spreading it evenly in the pan, and cook over the same *very* low heat for 45 to 50 minutes. During this time, your garlic nubbins will slowly begin to take on color, brown butter bits will coat the garlic, and magic will happen. Move the garlic around with a heatproof spatula, always leaving it in a nice, even layer. This takes time. At 35 minutes, you will probably think your garlic is good to go, but it's not; it still needs at least 15 more minutes to really, really, really caramelize.

2. Season with the salt off the heat. Let cool, and store in an airtight container in the fridge for up to 1 month.

Take the leek washing seriously. Those suckers can be very sandy.

CARAMELIZED LEEKS

MAKES ABOUT 1 CUP

Never had caramelized leeks? Your life is about to change. Mine did the first time I had them atop a Middle East–style pizza with cinnamon and nutmeg. I use them in the same way I do caramelized onions, but specifically when I'm looking for less sweetness to balance a dish and more complexity to give the perfect bite real legs. Though they bring less sweetness than caramelized onions, caramelized leeks tout a unique depth and a little more class.

1. With a sharp knife, cut 4 large leeks lengthwise in half. Wash away any sand or grit trapped between the leaves. Pat dry and then thinly slice crosswise, yielding small crescent-shaped slivers; use all of the whites and a small amount of the greens.

2. Follow the recipe for Caramelized Onions (page 159), adding 1 cup water to the sauté pan after the leeks have been cooking for about 20 minutes. By the time they're caramelized, the water will have hydrated the drier greener parts of the leeks and then evaporated.

SPREADABLE GARLIC

— MAKES ABOUT ½ CUP —

My sis and I used to make this killer condiment when we were in college, for an all-out college meal of focaccia with oven-roasted garlic spread on top. Now I also like to serve it with cheese plates and sliced roasted meat, to swirl it into bread dough before baking, and to spread it on toast.

5 heads garlic
5 teaspoons olive oil
1 teaspoon kosher salt

1. Heat the oven to 350°F.

2. With a sharp knife, cut off the top ⅛ inch of the garlic heads. Arrange the headless garlic bulbs in the center of a large sheet of aluminum foil, exposed cloves up. Drizzle a teaspoon of olive oil over each head, trying to get a little into each clove. Sprinkle the salt over the 5 heads. Seal the aluminum foil, making a tightly sealed package.

3. Bake for 2 hours. Let cool slightly and then while they are warm, pop the garlic cloves out of their skin and into an airtight container. Store in the refrigerator for up to a week.

MISO BUTTERSCOTCH SUNDAE

(BIG-BATCH STAPLE)

— SERVES 4 TO 6 —

When I was first navigating my way through creating desserts for the Momofuku restaurants, I made this concoction of intentionally burnt shiro miso (*shiro* means white; it's the most common type of miso) and other basic savory pantry ingredients. I was trying to create desserts that incorporated the restaurant's standard flavors, so there wouldn't be a huge disconnect between dinner and what came after it.

Knowing that toasting and browning give added depth and character to otherwise one-note flavors led me to this amazing sweet, salty, umami butterscotch-like spread that works equally well for a plated dessert as it does for *awesome* ice cream sundaes at home!

The sauce takes a few minutes to prepare, so I stock up on it when a freakin' weekend rolls around.

¼ **cup** shiro miso

4 **tablespoons (½ stick)** unsalted butter, at room temperature

¼ **cup packed** light brown sugar

¼ **cup** mirin

1 **teaspoon** sherry vinegar

1 **pint to 1 gallon** vanilla ice cream

GARNISH

toasted pecans, leftover Apple Dumplings (page 36), or just some cinnamon sugar

1. Heat the oven to 400°F.

2. Spread the miso in a thin even layer on a Silpat-lined or greased baking sheet and pop it in the oven for 10 to 15 minutes. The miso should be on the blackened side of browned (don't be a wuss) and have an appetizingly burnt aroma.

3. Let the miso cool briefly so it's easier to handle, then scrape it into a blender. Add the butter, brown sugar, mirin, and vinegar and blend until the mixture is homogenous and smooth. You've got miso butterscotch! Scrape it into a bowl, or store in the refrigerator, in an airtight container, for weeks.

4. Really need instructions to make a sundae? Fine! Grab bowls or fancy fluted glasses. Put a dollop of miso butterscotch in the bottom of each, then add a scoop of ice cream, a fun garnish, and repeat: miso butterscotch, ice cream, garnish. Build it high to the sky!

KODAK PORTRA 400   KODAK PORTRA 400   KODAK PORTRA 400

COOKOUT/ BONFIRE

We spend a *lot* of time indoors in the kitchen at Milk Bar, so when the weather is nice, we start to itch and scratch excitedly and make as many excuses as possible to open up a window, prop open a door, and let the fresh air in until quitting time, when we sprint out the door.

Though we're domesticated gals, we fancy ourselves outdoor women too. There's no sense in cooking when it's nice out if you're not doing it over an open flame! So warm weather means grilling in my backyard, on the roof of our kitchen (we've done it before and nearly got evicted!), or wherever the mood strikes. (Often we try to make it so we're near a beach when that mood is striking.) I'm an East Coast dame, so spring and summer also mean a bounty of produce that only comes with the warm weather—and is great on the grill. Everything tastes better smoked, caramelized, or charred.

But part of living life the Milk Bar way is celebrating it through every season, even fall

and winter—sometimes over the warmth of a bonfire! At its darkest, cold winter weather calls for preparing food that reminds me of better, warmer times. A Butter Burger (page 176) or Smoked Turkey Breast (page 182) will bring a warm grin year-round.

My favorite part of cooking outdoors is the snacking, grazing, and camaraderie that are part of it, and so the menu nearly always involves few rules and plenty of options to inspire the culinary genius and team player mentality in us all. You don't need much to host an outdoor (or indoor) feast, just a sense of spirit, some fresh foodstuffs, and some sweet/salty/tangy marinades. A cookout is also a great excuse to make funny, fancy drinks (see pages 194 to 198).

CHILLIN' & GRILLIN': TIPS & TRICKS

Many folks steer clear of cooking outdoors because they're unsure of the "right" way to do the deed. Here are some basic tips and tricks for when you are getting your grill or bonfire on. The secret is to play it cool when things start to heat up . . .

HOW TO FIRE UP YOUR GRILL

GAS: If you've got a gas grill (wuss), open up the flow of propane and press the ignite/light button. Cover and let heat for 10 minutes before using. Gas grills are decidedly more even and consistent in their heat distribution, but they fail to deliver that all-important smokiness that only burnt wood can provide.

CHARCOAL: I have a charcoal grill and I love it. (And, unlike in the 'burbs, there is next to nowhere you can buy propane in the city; I take back the wuss comment above if you can find some.) I recommend a chimney starter to get the coals going. It's a cheap piece of equipment and easy to use: Stuff some newspaper in the bottom, put the coals on top, set on the grates of your grill, and light the paper. When the coals have ashed over, remove the cooking grate from your grill and dump in the hot coals. Replace the cooking grate and lid, open the vents, and let the coals heat up the grill for about 5 minutes before grilling. (Think of it as preheating your oven.) If you're going to be grilling for a long period and/or have some big cuts of meat that will take more than half an hour or an hour, you'll need to replenish the coals from time to time. Just use the chimney starter again.

HOW TO MAN OR WOMAN A GRILL

Own your role as the grill master. Or, at the very least, fake it till you make it. Make sure you have tongs, a cold drink, and possibly a ridiculous apron or poufy chef's hat. Basically, if you're unsure how to act, pretend you're the Muppet Swedish Chef.

Using those tongs, transfer your bounty onto the cooking grate, arranging it with room for even heat distribution. Keep in mind that typically the center of the grill is a hot spot. Arrange anything delicate or small that will cook (or burn) quickly toward the outer part of the grill.

Once your grill is loaded, put the lid on. Wait 3 to 5 minutes, then check the underbelly of one of the small items for char lines. If they are not there yet, your grill is running

Keep your grill out of harm's way—make sure it is a safe distance from your house or shed, any brush, etc. I keep mine on a little stone and gravel ring I fashioned in my backyard, with a pail of salt or sand nearby, just in case.

Grill grates are easy to clean when hot. Get a wire brush and, if necessary, get to scrubbing before you fill your grill. Alternatively, set yourself up for success by scrubbing that sucker down post-grill, so you're ready to go next time.

a little cold and may need more time. Don't flip until you see those char marks! And don't get touchy! The more you touch, poke, prod, or move the items on the grill, the more you're breaking down their structure and releasing flavorful juices into the grill rather than onto your plate. You can hover, but hands off. Gently check on a single item every few minutes.

If you're grilling steak or other big cuts of meat, don't tear it off the grill. When it is happy and well cooked, it will release itself, just for you. Don't forget to let your grilled babies rest. Let those tasty juices settle before you cut in. This is also a great time to add more kosher salt or black pepper if you think something is underseasoned.

HOW TO BUILD A BONFIRE

Stake out your spot. Make sure it's legal. Whether you're on a beach or in a backyard, make sure you're far enough from people, places, or items that might catch on fire if things get rowdy.

Clear or dig a circle 1 to 3 feet across, depending on how big you want your bonfire. If you want to get fancy, arrange big dry stones, bricks, and/or rocks around the outer edges of the "pit." Grab the items to light on fire and arrange them in this order: First bunch together crumpled-up newspaper, twigs, and/or dry leaves in the center. Create a tepee shape above the small stuff with several logs. Light that baby up and burn, baby, burn, adding more logs as needed over time. Don't forget to put that sucker out with a pail of salt, sand, or water when it's bedtime.

SEASONING RAW MEAT

The mark of a great chef is salt control—knowing how much to add. Most home cooks are scared of adding too much, but chances are, whatever you're making can take twice as much salt as you think, especially if it's a thick cut of meat. Anytime you come across a recipe that says "salt to taste," do just that. If you are unsure how much salt to add, add what you think you'll like, then pinch or cut off a small amount, cook it, and taste it. If a flavor explosion doesn't erupt in your mouth, keep adding salt until it does—or until you are happy with the outcome (not everyone loves flavor explosions).

LEMON BARS

Nothing's better than a tart and tangy lemon bar. Though semilocal citrus is typically in season during the winter months, if you ask me, lemon bars are seasonless and always a home run after a smoky cookout or outdoor feast.

I've never found or conquered a from-scratch lemon bar that I've loved as much as one of my Nonna's, made with a little help from lemon cake mix. One of my favorite all-American bar cookies, they are great at room temp or straight out of the fridge or freezer.

butter for the baking dish

THE CRUST

1 (15-ounce) box lemon cake mix

8 tablespoons (1 stick) unsalted butter, melted

1 large egg

THE FILLING

⅓ cup lemon crust from above

½ pound cream cheese, at room temperature

2 cups confectioners' sugar

1 teaspoon kosher salt

2 lemons, zested and juiced

confectioners' sugar for dusting

1. Heat the oven to 350°F. Grease a 9 × 13-inch baking dish.

2. Make the crust: Beat together the cake mix, butter, and egg in the bowl of a stand mixer fitted with the paddle attachment (or in a mixing bowl, using a large wooden spoon) until homogenous. Scoop out ⅓ cup of the mixture and reserve for the filling. Dump the rest into the prepared dish and use your hands to press it firmly and evenly over the bottom.

3. Make the filling: Return the ⅓ cup reserved lemon crust to the mixing bowl and paddle it together with the cream cheese until the two have become one. Add the confectioners' sugar, salt, and lemon zest and juice and mix until well combined and smooth, 1 to 2 minutes. Use a spatula to spread the filling in an even layer on top of the lemon crust mixture.

4. Bake for 20 to 25 minutes, until the top has puffed slightly and is golden brown and beginning to crack. Cool completely.

5. Cut the lemon bars into 2-inch squares and dust with an even snowfall of confectioners' sugar. Cover with plastic and refrigerate for up to 1 week or freeze for up to 1 month.

MILK
BAR
RANCH
DIP

BEAN
DIP

BURNT-
HONEY-
MUSTARD
DIP

DIP LIFE

All great outdoor eating starts and ends with grazing, and the ne plus ultra of grazing foods are dips—for chips, raw vegetables, even fingers when no one is looking. Much as French cuisine has mother sauces, we milk maids and men enjoy our mother dips: bean, ranch, and burnt-honey-mustard. They are essential, elemental eating as well as fantastic building blocks for other dishes (the bean dip, for example, goes into Party Nachos, page 207; and Arepas, page 242).

BEAN DIP

MAKES ABOUT 4 CUPS

From Courtney McBroom, from Texas, to you, with love.

1 cup dried pinto or black beans

2 slices smoky bacon (like Benton's)
or 2 tablespoons rendered bacon fat

1 small yellow onion, diced
3 garlic cloves, chopped
½ jalapeño, seeded and chopped

4 cups water

1½ teaspoons kosher salt

1. Soak the beans overnight in 4 cups water. Drain the beans and rinse well.

2. Cook the bacon in a small pot (the one you will later cook the beans in) over medium heat until it has rendered its fat.

3. Remove the bacon, leaving the fat in the pot, and let cool slightly before chopping it fine. Return it to the pot. Add the onion, garlic, and jalapeño, turn the heat up to medium-high, and cook, stirring often, until the onion begins to soften and caramelize, about 10 minutes.

4. Add the beans and 4 cups water and bring to a boil. Reduce the heat to low and simmer, uncovered, until the beans are fully cooked and tender, about 1 hour. Stir occasionally, and add another splash or two of water or more if the pot begins to dry out. To test the beans, spoon one out of the pot and eat it; if it isn't completely soft, continue to simmer the beans until they are soft.

5. Add the salt and crank up the heat to medium-high to blast off any remaining liquid. Use a sturdy wooden spoon or a potato masher to stir the beans around and mash them up, until most of the liquid has evaporated and the beans are totally smashed. This will take about 10 minutes; you want the consistency to be that of a chunky thick porridge.

6. Turn the heat off and let the beans cool for 10 minutes. If you like bean dip a little chunky, it's done. If you want it smoooooooooooooth, blend it up. Serve at room temperature. The dip will keep in an airtight container in the fridge for up to a week.

BURNT-HONEY-MUSTARD DIP

MAKES 3 CUPS

Burnt honey was an accidental discovery I made back when I was in charge of the desserts at Momofuku Ko: I left a pot of honey on the stove too long and burnt it. I tasted it just as I was about to wash the pan out and found that it had taken on some crazy umami notes—and I actually found it more interesting than plain old honey!

I love making burnt-honey butter with it and using it on toast or in savory recipes such as Burnt-Honey-Butter Kale (page 106).

1 cup honey

1 cup plain yogurt
1 cup yellow mustard
1 teaspoon kosher salt
1 tablespoon honey

1. Pour the 1 cup honey into a medium saucepan, attach a candy thermometer to the pan, and cook over medium heat until the honey registers 325°F, about 10 minutes. The honey should be bubbly and deep brown, like no place you've ever taken a pot of honey before. Please be careful, because hot honey can burn the living daylights out of you.

2. Remove from the heat and whisk in the yogurt, mustard, salt, and the remaining 1 tablespoon honey (this is unburnt for a kick of sweetness). Chill in the fridge before serving. The dip will keep in an airtight container in the fridge for up to a week.

Got excess herbs in your garden or crisper drawer? Don't let 'em go to waste! You can dry and use them in this recipe or any recipe that calls for dried herbs. Set the oven to its lowest temp. Clean and dry the herbs, leaving the stems on. (Disembodied leaves blow away too easily.) Arrange the herbs on a lined baking sheet—use a Silpat or a kitchen

towel—as direct contact with a metal baking sheet will darken the color of the herbs. Turn the oven off, put the herbs in, and leave them in the oven for at least 4 hours, or overnight, until they're dry and brittle. Separate out and discard the stems and store the leaves in airtight containers at room temp for up to 6 months.

MILK BAR RANCH DIP

MAKES 2½ CUPS

After we'd used approximately our millionth gallon of Hidden Valley Ranch at Milk Bar, we decided to make our own version. As you must know, ranch is good on *everything*.

You could stop after step 1 and store the dry seasoning mix in an airtight container, to make mini batches of ranch on the fly, or to use as a seasoning mix. I love to rub down chicken wings with it before cooking or to add it to lima beans or any dried beans I breathe life into on the stovetop with water. Little Ball jars of ranch seasoning mix also make baller holiday gifts (remember to include instructions for animating it in the gift card).

¼ cup onion powder
¼ cup dried chives
3 tablespoons kosher salt
2 tablespoons garlic powder
1 tablespoon sugar
2½ teaspoons Colman's mustard powder
1 teaspoon black pepper
¾ teaspoon dried dill
½ teaspoon gochugaru (Korean red chili powder)
2 limes, zested

2 cups sour cream
½ cup buttermilk

1. Mix together the onion powder, chives, salt, garlic powder, sugar, mustard powder, pepper, dill, gochugaru, and lime zest in a small bowl.

2. Whisk together the sour cream and buttermilk in a medium bowl. Add the seasoning mix and stir until incorporated. Let sit in the fridge for at least 3 hours to develop flavor.

3. The dip will keep in an airtight container in the fridge for up to a week.

MARKY'S BUTTER BURGERS

— MAKES 4 BURGERS —

Brought to me (and you) by food stylist extraordinaire, baddest bass guitarist, and Kay & Ray's potato chip enthusiast Mark "Marky" Ibold, this is my *favorite* burger. A Wisconsin classic that takes me back to my teenage obsession with Wendy's burgers—crisp, juicy meat; soft, sweet bun; condiments galore—it's also the burger I make indoors year-round when I want to pretend it's nice enough outside to grill but it's not.

Martin's potato rolls are a must. If you're cooking for your lady friends, go smaller, maybe halfsies. If cooking for burly types, go bigger and double, maybe triple, this recipe. The most important thing is that you get the double-stack of burger—so don't skimp on the skyscraper effect. Have your condiments at the ready and your buns toasting while the meat is cooking. This is a good recipe to tackle with a friend, who can help keep things organized and dress the burgers while you're womanning the griddle, or vice versa. Let your inner diner cook trump your outer food snob and get a nice crisp char on your burgers rather than attempting to cook them medium-rare.

THE MEAT
1 pound ground beef

1 tablespoon kosher salt

2 teaspoons grapeseed or other neutral oil

THE ASSEMBLY
4 Martin's potato rolls, toasted

4 or more teaspoons mayonnaise, preferably Hellmann's

4 romaine or other sturdy-leaf lettuce leaves, cut or torn into burger-sized pieces

½ medium yellow onion, sliced into rings

1 medium tomato, sliced

½ cup crinkle-cut pickles

4 tablespoons (½ stick) unsalted butter, at room temperature

8 slices American cheese

1. Prep the meat: Divide the meat into 8 even portions and gently flatten each one into an ⅛-inch-thick patty. Season generously with the salt.

2. Slick a griddle or cast-iron skillet with a film of oil and get it good and hot over medium-high heat, 2 to 3 minutes.

3. Meanwhile, prep the buns: Put the buns in the toaster, or griddle-toast them in the pan before and during cooking the meat. (Remember, a spouse, a friend, or anyone over eight or so can help with this.)

4. Once the buns are toasty, accessorize them on a plate or platter:

   a. Spread 1 teaspoon mayonnaise, or more, on the bottom half of each bun.

b. Top with a few pieces of lettuce, a few onion rings, sliced tomatoes, and a smattering of pickles.

c. Smear 1 tablespoon of butter on the toasty underside of each bun top.

5. Add the patties to your now rip-roaringly hot griddle or pan, sear them on the first side until they're nice and brown and crusty, 2 or 3 minutes. Flip and top each patty with a slice of cheese. As soon as the cheese has gone gooey, stack 2 patties at a time on top of one another and spatula-transfer from the pan to their throne of condiments on the waiting dressed buns. Top with the buttered bun tops. Repeat as needed, and EAT!

CHOOSE-YOUR-OWN-ADVENTURE CHORIZO BURGERS

— MAKES 4 BURGERS —

Real-talk time: With the exception of Mark Ibold's Butter Burgers (page 176), plain old beef burgers never taste as good as I want them to. So I like to concoct my own flavorful numbers for the grill. I think of them as the Milk Bar take on those elaborate patties with fancy names (often evoking Florence or Morocco or some place where they don't eat burgers) that grocery stores make and sell for a ridiculous price.

I'm also—and by this point in the book, we probably know each other well enough that this is no surprise—a big fan of clean-out-the-fridge recipes. That's why this is a choose-your-own-adventure burger: whatever meat you want to eat is gonna work, whether lamb or ostrich, because you're going to season it like the tastiest meat loaf of your life (which makes this a good place to note that, in the too-cold-to-grill seasons, you could bake the results as a loaf instead of as patties).

And remember that this is a map, a mash-up: feel free to experiment with other leftover veggies (fennel would be great) and spices (do you have another rub you love? sub 6 tablespoons of it for the chorizo mix in the recipe). There's no need to have a grocery list a mile long to plan an adventure. The aim of this recipe is to make an unimpeachably delicious burger, freed from the disappointing and overly orthodox idea that plain beef is best.

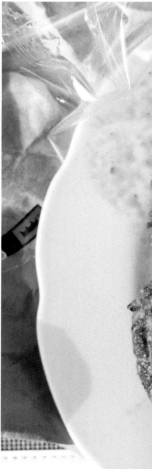

THE MIREPOIX

1 small carrot
1 celery stalk
¼ medium yellow onion

2 tablespoons grapeseed or other neutral oil

2 garlic cloves
¼ teaspoon kosher salt

THE CHORIZO SPICE RUB

2 tablespoons chili powder
1 tablespoon paprika
1 tablespoon kosher salt
1 tablespoon onion powder
2 teaspoons crushed red pepper flakes
1½ teaspoons garlic powder

1½ teaspoons ground cumin
¼ teaspoon ground coriander
¼ teaspoon black pepper
1 lime, zested

THE MEAT

4 strips thick-cut bacon
1 pound ground meat (any mix of beef, pork, veal, turkey, and/or sausage)

¼ teaspoon jarred horseradish
1 tablespoon Worcestershire sauce
1 large egg

THE FIXINS

4 to 8 slices cheese of your choice
condiments of your choosing, including mayonnaise
4 hamburger buns

The chorizo spice rub is awesome on any and every meat recipe. Make larger batches of it and jar it up for future cooking adventures or gift it away any time of year.

1. Prep the mirepoix: Dice the carrot, celery, and onion into small squares, approximately ¼ inch.

2. Heat the oil in a medium skillet over medium heat until it is shimmering but not smoking, then add the carrot, celery, and onion. Sauté the veggies until softened, about 10 minutes.

3. Smash the garlic cloves with the side of a knife, give them a rough chop, and throw them into the pan. Add the salt and continue to cook, stirring often, until the veggies are broken down, about 10 minutes. Remove from the heat and set aside to cool.

4. Meanwhile, prep the chorizo spice rub: Combine the chili powder, paprika, salt, onion powder, red pepper flakes, garlic powder, cumin, coriander, pepper, and lime zest in a small bowl, stirring until everything is evenly mixed. Set aside.

5. Heat your grill (see page 166).

6. Prep the meat: Cut the bacon into ¼-inch-wide strips (aka batons). Combine with the ground meat in a mixing bowl. (If you're using sausages, open them up by running the tip of your knife down the casing and then push out the loose meat.) Add the horseradish, Worcestershire sauce, egg, cooled veggies, and the spice mix to the bowl o' meat and mush the mess together with your hands. Don't be afraid to get dirty.

7. Divide the meat into 4 even portions and shape into balls. Flatten those balls into patties about ½ inch thick (feel free to make them thicker, or thinner, according to your taste buds).

8. Cook the burgers for 4 to 5 minutes on each side; they should get a nice color and cook through (timing and doneness will depend on the mash-up of proteins you choose).

9. Use the fixins: Top the burgers with your choice of cheese and cook until the burgers are firm but not hard to the touch and the cheese has gotten warm and melty. Add whatever fixins you like on a burger and slap a bun on either side of each one. TA-DA!

SMOKED TURKEY BREAST

— SERVES 6, WITH LEFTOVERS —————————————

I can't tell you how many holidays my sister and I plotted our turkey attack, every year looking for a bigger, badder preparation than the year before. Brine it? Rub it? Fry it?

Sis finally married up from me and inherited not only a stand-up man, but also a partner in crime in the kitchen with some sky-high recipes, including this one, which is now our gold standard. We will search no further when it comes to turkey preparation. You can, of course, smoke a whole bird using this technique, but there's no sense in waiting until the holidays to fire up some wood chips, and I often make this smaller recipe.

¼ **cup packed** dark brown sugar
¼ **cup** kosher salt
2 tablespoons black pepper

1 (8-pound) boneless turkey breast

6 cups wood chips

1. Mix together the sugar, salt, and pepper in a small bowl.

2. Put the turkey in a pan large enough to hold it and shower that bird with the sugar mixture, then rub the mixture into the skin and the cavity to ensure that every part of it gets seasoned.

3. It's best to follow the manufacturer's instructions for proper smoking procedure, but this is how I do it with my Big Chief Smoker: Put the seasoned turkey on the bottom rack of the smoker. Add some wood chips to the "chip holder" (technical term) and fire up your smoker (or grill) to smoke for 4 hours, checking the wood chip (and charcoal, if applicable) supply every hour. I start with 3 cups wood chips and add another 3 cups over the course of the 4 hours.

4. The turkey is done when a meat thermometer inserted into the breast reads 160°F. Let sit for 20 minutes, then dive in.

SMOKED TURKEY SALAD

— MAKES ABOUT 6 CUPS; SERVES MANY —

I rarely come across a recipe for anything other than a baked good that I'm willing to stalk someone for. This recipe is an exception; I had to tease it out of my brother-in-law's stepfather, a raucous Floridian pit master named Wild Bill. I fell in love with it (and him) because of its smoky, sweet ease and its mayonnaise binding, as any good girl from the cornfields of Ohio would.

It's an awesome way to church up some Thanksgiving or Christmas or any other turkey dinner leftovers. I love smoked turkey in this recipe, but roasted or deep-fried turkey works too. Serve with crusty bread or slices of white bread, or heck, crackers, and cold beer. Eating it with a spoon out of the bowl late at night is also an acceptable serving technique.

4 pounds pulled Smoked Turkey Breast (page 182)

1 (16-ounce) jar sweet pickles, drained and chopped

OR

1½ cups sweet pickle relish, not drained

1½ cups pecans, toasted and roughly chopped

1 small red onion, diced

1 to 1½ cups mayonnaise (just enough to bind), preferably Hellmann's

Put the pulled turkey in a large bowl. Add the pickles, pecans, onion, and mayo and stir it all together.

The secret to this recipe is the sweet, acidic relish. No relish? No problem! Pulse your favorite supermarket or homemade pickled vegetables into a relish-like state in a food processor and substitute.

Fowl Wisdom: If you want to soar with eagles, don't hang with turkeys!

BBQ SO-EASY SAUCE

— MAKES ABOUT 1½ CUPS —

If something tastes good—like root beer, or Ritz crackers, or the combination of peas and strawberries—it will taste good as an ice cream. I truly believe this.

This sauce is Courtney McBroom's baby, and I fell in love with it so hard that I decided to turn it into a soft-serve flavor at the East Village Milk Bar during the summer of 2010. (It was in good company, with creamed-corn soft serve and purple-drink soft serve.) I'm pretty sure she and I were the only two who ever ate it. In fact, "BBQ Soft Serve" has since become accepted shorthand at Milk Bar menu development meetings for a weird, off-the-cuff idea that probably won't work. Whatever. I have no regrets.

The world wasn't ready for this BBQ so-easy sauce in ice cream form, but you're guaranteed to love it as a trusty grilling companion!

1 tablespoon olive oil

1 small yellow onion, diced
pinch of light brown sugar
½ teaspoon kosher salt, or more if needed

¼ cup ketchup (I fancy Heinz)

¼ cup molasses
¼ cup packed light brown sugar
¼ cup sherry vinegar
1 tablespoon Colman's mustard powder
2 teaspoons Worcestershire sauce
¼ teaspoon ground cumin

1. Heat the oil in a medium skillet over medium heat. Add the onion, along with the brown sugar and salt, cover, and cook, stirring occasionally, until the onion goes soft and translucent, 15 or so minutes.

2. Turn the heat down to medium-low (keep it more on the low side) and cook for another 30 minutes, stirring enough to allow the onion to caramelize in the pan without sticking and burning, until it is deep brown, soft, and sweet. You will know it's ready after you have a taste and can't help but say, "Oh, DAMN!" Be patient—this process takes time.

3. While the onion is cooking, whisk together the ketchup, molasses, ¼ cup brown sugar, vinegar, mustard powder, Worcestershire sauce, and cumin in a bowl. Stir to dissolve the sugar.

4. Once the onion has reached the "Oh, DAMN!" stage, stir it into the BBQ sauce you just made. Taste and add more salt if needed. The sauce can be used immediately, but it gets even better after it's had a few days to develop flavor in the fridge. Store in an airtight container, as such, for up to a month.

PUT IT ON A STICK:
THROW A SHISH KEBAB PARTY!

Shish kebabs are a great way to make your friends cook for themselves. Almost anything can be skewered or grilled, and everyone likes food on a stick.

A few guidelines for a successful shish kebab party:

- Soak bamboo skewers in water for 2 hours or overnight. (If you have metal skewers, well, then, you are fancier than I am.)
- Marinate anything that needs marinating.
- Have all the vegetables and meats cut and prepped before you start building skewers.
- Oil and salt everything before it hits the grill. Oil is a conduit of heat: if it's not oiled, it won't grill as well or as fast as you want it to. And salt = flavor.
- Meditate on a few deconstructed kebab themes to match your party: sports (chicken wing, chicken wing, chicken wing), Francophile (cubed baguette, ham, Swiss), New Yorker (cabbage/sauerkraut, brisket slathered in spicy mustard, cubes of rye bread). Or just follow some of my other favorites below.

Classic Midwestern
beef, potato, onion, beef, potato, onion
Use any kind of beef chunks here, marinated in one of the marinades on pages 188 to 191. For the fingerling potatoes and pearl onions, fill a medium pot with water and bring it to a boil. Add the fingerlings and boil until they offer just the barest resistance to the tip of a sharp knife, about 5 minutes. Remove from the pot with a slotted spoon. Drop in the onions and boil for 2 to 3 minutes. Remove from the pot, drain well, and slide them out of their skins. Once the potatoes are cool enough to handle, slice them in half and toss to coat with olive oil, salt, and pepper.

All-American
bun, hot dog, dill pickle, red onion, hot dog, bun
Slice hot dogs on a diagonal into 1½-inch pieces. Slice red onions into wedges. Brush Martin's potato rolls with butter and season with salt and pepper, then cut each half into 4 pieces.

Mediterranean
lemon wedge, tilapia fillet or small chunk, green olive, green olive, green olive, tilapia, lemon wedge

Dessert
buttered/sugared cubes o' bread/doughnut/ muffin/cake, fruit chunks (pineapple, bananas, peaches), citrus wedges

MARINADES

Meat wants to be marinated. (So do vegetables, a lot of the time.)

So give it what it wants: submerge the object of your affection in one of these marinades, cover the bowl with plastic or a tight-fitting lid, and refrigerate for a minimum of 4 hours, or up to 24 hours, depending on size and cut. Remember that maximum flavor comes with time.

Most proteins work well in many marinades, but here is a list of my favorites:

- Shrimp (peel and eat) in Chile-Lime-Soy Marinade
- Beef in Chile-Lime-Soy Marinade or Yogurt-Sriracha Marinade
- Pork of any shape or size in Cubano Marinade
- Chicken or turkey in Yogurt-Sriracha Marinade

CUBANO

MAKES ABOUT 3 CUPS

This is not a sissy marinade: it's wildly robust and will punch you in the face if you're not ready for it. We worked backward on it when we wanted to roast some pork Cuban style but couldn't get enough flavor to penetrate the meat. Finally we turned up the flavor volume with an ungodly amount of garlic and cumin.

1½ **cups** orange juice (store-bought is fine)
1½ **cups** lemon juice
2 **tablespoons** dried oregano
2½ **tablespoons** ground cumin
10 garlic cloves, roughly chopped

Whisk together all of the ingredients in a large bowl.

Technically
marination is the process of soaking food in a seasoned, often acidic, liquid before cooking. But guess what? These marinades are also awesome as *laterades*. Made fresh (read: they haven't bathed any raw proteins), they really turn up the volume and flavor of shredded cooked meat, which otherwise has a tendency to dry out.

CHILE-LIME-SOY

MAKES ABOUT 2 CUPS

David Chang has taught me a great deal, and though I've worked for many chefs, I've never met anyone else who has influenced me so strongly in terms of staple ingredients and the balance of flavor they provide. In nearly every dish I've seen him prepare, he seasons and balances flavors as needed with the following pantry staples:

sweet: apple juice or cider, light brown sugar, onion
spice/heat: garlic, Thai chile pepper, black pepper, Dijon mustard
salt: soy sauce
acid: lime, garlic, Dijon mustard

This marinade is my go-to. It's sweet, spicy, salty, and acidic and makes everything it touches that much better.

½ **cup** apple juice or cider
½ **cup** soy sauce, such as Kikkoman
¼ **cup packed** light brown sugar
½ **small** yellow onion, chopped
1 Thai or other small red chile pepper, seeded and sliced
3 limes, zested and juiced
2 garlic cloves, minced
2 **tablespoons** grapeseed or other neutral oil
1 **teaspoon** Dijon mustard
1 **teaspoon** black pepper

Whisk together all of the ingredients in a large bowl.

YOGURT-SRIRACHA

MAKES 1¾ CUPS

Do your best Valley Girl impression: say "Sriracha is *SO HOT* right now."

1 cup plain yogurt
½ cup buttermilk
3 tablespoons Sriracha sauce
2 tablespoons fish sauce
1 tablespoon chopped fresh mint leaves
1 lime, zested and juiced

Whisk together all of the ingredients in a large bowl.

CHICKEN WINGS + ANY MARINADE

— SERVES 4 —

If you want to baste your wings as they cook, to avoid a salmonella party, either make extra marinade or bring the marinade the wings soaked in to a good rolling boil and boil for a minute before using.

1½ pounds chicken wings
marinade of your choice (pages 188 to 191)

kosher salt

1. Add the chicken wings to the marinade and marinate for up to 24 hours in the fridge. If possible, toss from time to time.

2. Grill the wings over medium-high heat (color = flavor when dealing with wings), brushing with more marinade, if desired, until the wings are cooked through and on the blackened side of browned. Season with salt to taste.

MANGRIA

— SERVES 4 TO 6 —

For sangria-soaked backyard soirees in the warmer months, I like to turn the fruit up a notch by throwing it on the grill first, to let its flavors really reveal themselves over the flames. This adds great smoky and caramelized notes to the fruit, and therefore to the corresponding wine it's mixed with. Anything smoky is manly to a gaggle of giggling girls. Hence the *man*-gria.

2 plums
2 nectarines
1 apricot
1 mango
¼ pineapple
2 (750-ml) bottles white wine
up to ¼ cup sugar or honey, if needed

1. Soak bamboo skewers for 2 hours or overnight in water.

2. Make a fire in your grill (see page 166).

3. Clean and pit the fruit as necessary, then slice and skewer. Grill until the fruit is good and charred, 3 to 5 minutes over a hot fire or 10 to 15 minutes over a weak one that's already fired off a round of burgers. Let cool.

4. Pour the wine into a pitcher. Mash the fruit into smaller pieces and add to the wine. Sweeten if needed. Serve over ice.

Feel free to make your own version of mangria with any wine you have lingering in your house, and with any fruit you can slice up and grill for the occasion.

You can be a wine snob and purposefully select a baller bottle of wine to debase, but Barefoot 1.5-L white wine bottles do just fine too—ripe for the degradation.

Add a splash of whiskey, gin, mulled wine, or spirit for a little more depth and "perspective."

À LA MINUTE 'BRUSCO

— SERVES 4 —

Spring and summer make me feel effervescent. And, in turn, I want to consume all things effervescent.

But I can only take so much champagne and prosecco (it gets a little too sweet for even my sweet tooth), and only a few wine stores, even in the hip 'hoods that have wine stores, carry Lambrusco, a slightly fizzy Italian red wine.

So in my desperation-party-planning mode (when the most creative work is typically done), I make à la minute Lambrusco with any type of wine, preferably red, in my SodaStream soda maker. Focus on the haves, not the have-nots (I'm pretty sure my mom taught me that). Even Franzia turns into an incredibly refreshing way to pass a few hours in a Brooklyn backyard.

1 (750-ml) bottle whatever wine you got; if it's chilled, even better

Fill the bottle for your soda maker to the designated line, lock the canister in place, and carbonate!

MIMOSA SHMIMOSA

— SERVES 4 TO 6 —

Grilling out ain't no baby shower or ladies' luncheon, but sometimes you gotta get the grill started early and need a little wakey-wakey to celebrate the event. So treat yo'self with a mimosa alternative.

1 (750-ml) bottle sparkling rosé (to make your own, see À la Minute 'Brusco, opposite)

4 cups grapefruit juice

Splash equal parts rosé and grapefruit juice into champagne flutes, Solo cups, or any other drinking receptacles. Add ice cubes if you forgot to refrigerate either or if it's an especially hot morning.

ARNIE PALMER

— SERVES 4 TO 6 —

I *love* **the balance** of bittersweet, tannin-y tea with bittersweet citrus juice in an Arnold Palmer. I've turned this classic combo into everything from a palate-cleansing sorbet to a jelly to be layered in a tea cake. Using a variety of citrus juices other than lemon makes this my favorite homage to this classy golfer's beverage!

2 cups water
1 Lipton tea bag

½ cup sugar
¾ cup water
4 limes, juiced
¼ cup Ruby Red grapefruit juice
2 tablespoons bottled yuzu juice (available at amazon.com or a Japanese market; it's shelf-stable!)
⅛ teaspoon kosher salt

1. Bring the 2 cups water to a boil in a small saucepan over high heat. Remove the pan from the stove, add the tea bag, and let steep, covered, for 30 minutes.

2. Discard the tea bag, add the sugar to the tea, and stir until dissolved. Add the ¾ cup water, the lime juice, grapefruit juice, yuzu juice, and salt, stirring to dissolve the salt. Serve over ice.

ARNIE PALMER 'CHELADAS

We love micheladas (a Mexican beer sprucer-upper of *cerveza* with lime juice, chili powder, and salt), we love our Arnie Palmers, and they both contain lime—so why not love them both at the same time?

¼ **cup** kosher salt
1 teaspoon chili powder

1 lime, cut into 4 wedges

4 (12-ounce) bottles Pacifico or any light beer
1 cup Arnie Palmer (page 197)

1. Combine the salt and chili powder on a small plate. Rub the rims of plastic Solo cups or beer steins with the lime wedges and dredge them in the chili salt.

2. Fill the glasses three-quarters full with beer, then top off with the Arnie Palmer. Add ice, garnish with the lightly used lime wedges, and serve.

CRAFT NIGHT/ SLEEP OVER

You are never too old for a craft night with old friends and new friends, little friends and big friends. Supermodel friends too!

I like to make sure my craft nights run late, because any excuse for a slumber party is a good one. I live for the hijinks that ensue, whether I'm keeping a gaggle of kids up past their bedtimes or drinking wine with my girlfriends. The occasional sleepover keeps a person young and goofy. I love to bring crafts to a slumber party, because you can never underestimate the bonds that friendship bracelets, Krazy Glue, and glitter can make.

So pack a bag with your silly pj's and your grandma's knitting needles and don't forget to bring this book!

The chapter is divided into two sections, Night Owls and Early Birds.

Night Owls has recipes for snacks to get you and your pals through a scary movie night, along with craft-style recipes that you can make as an activity. (And give as gifts or party favors afterward.) Early Bird recipes are for the morning after a slumber paaaarrrrrrt*aaaaaaaay*!!!!!!!!!!!!!!

LIME, YOGURT, AND OLIVE OIL CAKE

— MAKES 1 (9 × 5-INCH) LOAF; SERVES 8 TO 12 ————

This recipe can be made for dessert the night of or breakfast the next morning, or as cute gifts to send guys and gals home with or give away.

You *must* use olive oil in this cake. And it needs to be fancy olive oil, to boot. Most of the flavor in this cake comes from it, so don't skimp; get yourself a bottle of the tasty stuff.

THE CAKE

1 cup full-fat Greek yogurt
½ cup fancy olive oil
1 cup granulated sugar
3 limes, 3 zested, 2 juiced

2 large eggs
1 large egg yolk

1¾ cups all-purpose flour
1 teaspoon baking powder
½ teaspoon baking soda
1¼ teaspoons kosher salt

THE GLAZE

1 cup confectioners' sugar
3 limes, 3 zested, 2 juiced
1 tablespoon fancy olive oil

1. Heat the oven to 350°F. Grease a 9 × 5-inch loaf pan.

2. Make the cake: Whisk together the yogurt, olive oil, granulated sugar, and lime zest and juice in a large bowl until combined. Add the eggs and yolk and whisk them in too. (This should be done by hand; it's about gently combining the ingredients, not beating them together.)

3. Add the flour, baking powder, baking soda, and salt, mixing until just combined. Take care not to overwork the batter, as every unneeded stir takes your batter farther from perfectly tender and closer to a sad, dense brick.

4. Pour the batter into the greased pan. Bake for 40 to 50 minutes, until the top is golden brown and a tester inserted into the middle comes out clean.

5. While the cake is in the oven, make the glaze: Whisk together the confectioners' sugar, lime zest and juice, and olive oil in a small bowl.

6. Once the cake has baked, let it cool in the pan for 5 minutes, then invert and put it right side up on a serving platter. While the cake is still warm, pour the glaze evenly over the top and sides. The cake will be moist and slightly sticky. Serve warm, at room temperature, or cold.

Fold 1 cup fresh or dried blueberries into the batter right before baking to achieve a blueberry muffin effect.

The batter makes great actual muffins. Bake in muffin tins lined with cupcake papers for 10 to 12 minutes.

Going the gift route? Bake the batter in a bunch of aluminum foil mini loaf pans. Leave the loaves in their pans once baked and drizzle the glaze on top. Once they have cooled, put them in cellophane bags and tie the bags with string or friendship bracelets.

KIMCHEEZ-ITS WITH BLUE CHEESE DIP

— SERVES 4 TO 6 —

Cheez-Its are a thing of beauty, especially when you're late-night snacking with gal pals. Because we challenge all great late-night snacking with a sense of "from scratch" wonder, we just had to challenge how in the world they packed all that cheddar into those little cheesy crackers. We took our results to a whole other level with the help of sweet, spicy, fermented kimchi, a required refrigerator ingredient if you're in the Momofuku family.

1 cup kimchi (store-bought or homemade)

¾ pound cheddar cheese, shredded

1⅓ cups all-purpose flour
1 packet (¼ cup) cheddar powder
¼ teaspoon cayenne pepper

Blue Cheese Dip (recipe follows)

1. Put the kimchi in a strainer lined with cheesecloth set over a bowl and let it drain in the refrigerator for 1 to 2 hours.

2. Heat the oven to 250°F.

3. Remove the kimchi from the strainer and discard the liquid (or use it to make kimchi Bloody Marys!). Put the drained kimchi in a food processor and puree it until it's completely smooth.

4. Combine the kimchi puree and shredded cheddar in the bowl of a stand mixer fitted with the paddle attachment and cream together until very smooth, about 3 minutes. Scrape the bowl down with a spatula, add the flour, cheddar powder, and cayenne, and mix until the dry ingredients are fully incorporated, about 30 seconds. Scrape the bowl down again and mix on low for an additional minute. The dough will be very stiff. If it's too much for your mixer, finish kneading it by hand.

5. Divide the dough into 6 portions and shape into balls. Put each ball between two sheets of parchment or wax paper and, using a rolling pin, roll it to a cracker-like thinness, about ⅛ inch.

BLUE CHEESE DIP
MAKES 2 CUPS

2 tablespoons dried chives
2 tablespoons onion powder
1 tablespoon kosher salt
2 teaspoons garlic powder
½ teaspoon black pepper
½ teaspoon sugar
⅛ teaspoon dried dill

1 cup sour cream
¼ cup mayonnaise, preferably Kewpie
1 tablespoon white vinegar

¼ pound good blue cheese, such as Stilton, crumbled

1. Mix the dried chives, onion powder, salt, garlic powder, pepper, sugar, and dried dill in a small bowl.

2. Whisk together the sour cream, mayo, and vinegar in a medium bowl. Add the seasoning mix and stir until completely incorporated. Stir in the blue cheese, smashing it a little along the way to break it down.

3. Let the dip sit for at least 3 hours in the fridge to develop flavor. It will keep in an airtight container in the fridge for up to a week.

6. Remove the top piece of paper from each dough round and then, using a paring knife or a pizza cutter, cut the dough into 1-inch squares. You should get about 40 small crackers from each round. Transfer to greased or lined baking sheets. You will need about one baking sheet per dough round; bake them off in batches.

7. Bake the crackers for 15 minutes. Reduce the oven temperature to 180°F and bake for another 8 minutes, or until the crackers are completely dry and just starting to brown on the edges. Cool completely.

8. Serve with the blue cheese dip.

You can buy cheddar powder at Amazon or kingarthurflour.com. It's the same stuff that comes in packets in boxed macaroni and cheese!

Top the nachos with the works only if you're sure people are ready to eat. If you are dealing with a crowd of picky eaters or grazers, keep the post-oven toppings on the side and deploy them as "dippins." You don't want things to get soggy and gross.

PARTY NACHOS

— SERVES 6 —

Similar to the Choose-Your-Own-Adventure Chorizo Burgers (page 178), and a world away from Desperation Nachos (page 132), this is my improvement on a dish that has so much potential but is so often underwhelming. Take the recipe as more baseline than bible, and build your own tower of crunch.

The key to great nachos is spreading them out in a thin-enough layer so that every chip (or almost every chip) has some form of topping on it. Nothing makes me angrier than a pile of nachos with delicious cheese and filling *only on the chips that are lucky enough to be on top*. Brutal.

1 (13-ounce) bag tortilla chips

1 (10.5-ounce) bag Fritos Scoops (Scoops are *essential*)

6 cups shredded or grated cheese, such as a mixture of Monterey Jack, sharp cheddar, and cotija (about 1½ pounds)

1 (16-ounce) can refried beans or 2 cups Bean Dip (page 174)

1 (15.5-ounce) can black beans, drained

½ **pound** ground meat, cooked with a packet of taco seasoning

1 poblano pepper, seeded and cut into thin strips

1 medium Spanish onion, chopped

1 (16-ounce) jar taco sauce (I like Ortega brand)

1½ cups tomato salsa

2 cups sour cream

1 (12-ounce) jar pickled sliced jalapeños, drained

6 scallions, thinly sliced

2 ears corn, kernels removed

2 avocados, halved, pitted, peeled, and thinly sliced

1 cup loosely packed fresh cilantro leaves

1. Set the oven to broil.

2. Arrange the chips and Scoops in a single layer on a baking sheet or in your largest baking dish, ensuring an even distribution of chips and Scoops. (If necessary, divide them between two baking dishes.)

3. Shower the chips with the cheese. This will act as a crucial moisture barrier to protect them from everything else. Add the two types of beans. Next up, scatter the meat evenly over the beans. Top that with the poblano and onion, scattered evenly for optimum flavor distribution.

4. Pop the whole mess under the broiler until the cheese is melted and starting to brown around the edges. This happens fast—3 to 5 minutes—so keep watch!

5. Remove the baking sheet from the oven and top the nachos with the taco sauce, salsa, sour cream, jalapeños, scallions, corn, avocado, and cilantro, evenly distributed, *of course*. Serve immediately.

LATE-NIGHT JAM-AND-JELLY SESH

If you are interested in learning the craft of canning, jarring, and preserving, then I don't think you're ready for this jelly.

Please refer to any of the hundreds of lovely books on the subject; this is not one of them. I'm not trying to keep my cupboards stocked for the winter—I just wanna make some respectable jams and jellies, and eat them this week or next on sammies, toast, or cake. They also make great gifts for sharing with my girlfriends.

You can put them in cute 2-ounce jars or Tupperware or any vessel of your choosing.

PICKLED-STRAWBERRY JAM

MAKES ABOUT 2 CUPS

We use this recipe in all sorts of iterations at Milk Bar. It's sweet and tangy and supremely excellent. The smaller and redder the strawberries, the higher the quality and deeper the flavor.

1 cup ripe strawberries, hulled, pureed, and strained
½ **cup** sugar
2 tablespoons sherry vinegar
1½ **tablespoons** white wine vinegar

1 teaspoon powdered pectin
½ **cup** sugar

¼ **teaspoon** kosher salt
pinch of black pepper
½ **cup** strawberries, hulled and quartered (optional)

1. Whisk together the strawberry puree, ½ cup sugar, and both vinegars in a medium saucepan and warm over medium heat until hot to the touch.

2. Whisk the pectin with ½ cup sugar in a small bowl to combine, then whisk into the warming strawberry mixture. Bring to a boil, then reduce the heat and simmer for 2 to 3 minutes to ensure that the pectin is fully hydrated.

3. Stir in the salt, pepper, and quartered strawberries if you please, and simmer for 1 minute more, or until the strawberries have softened. Let cool.

4. Portion the jam out into jars. Keep refrigerated, and eat within 2 weeks.

If you're averse to being a jam or jelly person, at least be a compound-butter gal or guy. When paddled with room-temperature butter and a pinch of salt, all of these jams and jellies make fantastic flavored butters to jar and give away. My go-to ratio is 8 tablespoons (1 stick) unsalted butter to ¼ cup jam or jelly, with a pinch of salt. Paddle in ½ cup confectioners' sugar too, and you have a great frosting.

BLUEBERRY MISO JELLY

MAKES ABOUT 2 CUPS

The miso lends a surprising umami note to this jelly, and the blueberries keep it fresh. It is one of my favorite flavor combos, great in a smoothie or warmed and drizzled over an ice cream sundae.

2 tablespoons shiro miso

1 pint blueberries, pureed and strained
½ cup sugar
1 tablespoon rice vinegar

1 teaspoon powdered pectin
½ cup sugar

1. Put the miso in a small saucepan, set over medium heat, and, with a heatproof spatula, toss the miso around and toast, stirring often, until it is dark brown and fragrant, about 5 minutes.

2. Add the blueberry puree, ½ cup sugar, and the vinegar, and whisk together, making sure to get all of the toasted miso off the bottom of the pan, and then warm over medium heat until the mixture is hot to the touch.

3. Whisk the pectin with ½ cup sugar in a small bowl to combine, then whisk into the warming blueberry mixture. Bring to a boil, then reduce the heat and simmer for 2 to 3 minutes to ensure that the pectin is fully hydrated. Let cool.

4. Portion the jelly out into jars. Keep refrigerated, and eat within 2 weeks.

SMOKED-CANTALOUPE JAM

MAKES ABOUT 2 CUPS

Save this bad mama jamma for the summer months, when cantaloupe is in season and fragrant. Make sure you use a melon that is so ripe that the outer shell is nearly mush.

½ cantaloupe, as ripe as can be

3 teaspoons powdered pectin
½ cup sugar
½ teaspoon kosher salt

1. Seed the cantaloupe half. Scoop out the flesh with a spoon and put it in a heatproof container. Smoke it for 15 minutes.

2. Put the cantaloupe in a medium saucepan and heat over medium heat until warm to the touch. At this point the cantaloupe will still be chunky. (It will break down in step 3.)

3. Whisk the pectin with the sugar and salt in a small bowl to combine, then whisk into the warming cantaloupe. Bring to a boil, then reduce the heat and simmer for 2 to 3 minutes to ensure that the pectin is fully hydrated. Let cool.

4. Portion the jam out into jars. Keep refrigerated, and eat within 2 weeks.

I'm not a smoker anymore, so now when I smoke, I use a Big Chief Smoker! (Joke, Mom, JOKE!) You can get smoking done a lot of different ways. My brothers like to do what they call "grill smoking": They take wood chips, set them on fire, and put them in a grill (turned off) along with the protein or produce they want to smoke for up to 2 hours. If you don't have wood chips or a smoker, or a clue about smoking, make this recipe sans smoke.

ROSEMARY JELLY

MAKES ABOUT 2 CUPS

This is awesome on toasty bread with ricotta or mozzarella, or over a bowl of vanilla ice cream.

¾ **cup** water

1 tablespoon fresh rosemary leaves (about 2 sprigs)

½ **cup** sugar

2 tablespoons cider vinegar

¾ **teaspoon** powdered pectin

½ **cup** sugar

½ **teaspoon** kosher salt

1 drop green food coloring (optional)

1. Bring the water to a boil in a small saucepan. Add the rosemary, give it a stir, and remove from the heat. Cover the pan and let steep for 15 minutes.

2. Strain the liquid and discard the rosemary. You should have ¾ cup liquid; if you don't, add water to reach that amount. Return the rosemary liquid to the pan and whisk in ½ cup sugar and the vinegar. Heat over medium heat until warm to the touch.

3. Whisk the pectin with ½ cup sugar and the salt in a small bowl to combine, then whisk into the warming rosemary liquid. Bring to a boil, then reduce the heat and simmer for 2 to 3 minutes to ensure that the pectin is fully hydrated.

4. Remove the jelly from the heat and skim off any foam. Stir in the food coloring if you want it to be green (it's prettier that way). Let cool.

5. Portion the jelly out into jars. Keep refrigerated, and eat within 2 weeks.

FINES-HERBES JELLY

You can use any herb combo you like in place of the rosemary. I go for 2 teaspoons each chopped fresh parsley, tarragon, marjoram, and chervil. Proceed as for Rosemary Jelly.

PEPPER JAM

MAKES ABOUT 2 CUPS

This works great in the Zucchini Parm sandwich (page 240). It's also delicious mixed with a little cream cheese and salsa and eaten as a dip with corn chips.

3 large green bell peppers, cored, seeded, and roughly chopped
3 jalapeño peppers, seeded and roughly chopped

¾ cup cider vinegar

½ cup sugar

2 teaspoons powdered pectin
½ cup sugar
½ teaspoon kosher salt

2 jalapeño peppers, seeded and diced

1. Toss the bell peppers and chopped jalapeños into the food processor and pulse until finely chopped.

2. Transfer the chopped peppers to a medium saucepan and stir in the cider vinegar. Bring the mixture to a boil, then reduce the heat and simmer for 15 minutes.

3. Line a fine-mesh sieve with cheesecloth and set it over a bowl. Strain the pepper liquid into the bowl and discard the peppers. You should have about ½ cup liquid; if you have a lot more than that, put the liquid back on the stove and reduce it to ½ cup. Or, if you have less, add water to make ½ cup.

4. Return the liquid to the saucepan and whisk in ½ cup sugar. Heat over medium heat until warm to the touch.

5. Whisk the pectin with ½ cup sugar and the salt in a small bowl to combine, then whisk into the warming pepper liquid. Bring to a boil, then reduce the heat and simmer for 2 to 3 minutes to ensure that the pectin is fully hydrated.

6. Remove the jelly from the heat and skim off any foam. Stir in the diced jalapeños, then stir as the jelly cools to keep the fresh pepper bits suspended throughout.

7. Portion the jam out into jars. Keep refrigerated, and eat within 2 weeks.

Use half pickled and half fresh jalapeños for a twist. You can also use banana peppers or peperoncini.

OLIVE JAM

MAKES ABOUT 2 CUPS

Most people will probably skip this recipe because they think it will be too strange. Don't be one of those people. The saltiness of the olives and the sweetness of the sugar go together just right: didn't you ever dip your French fries into your milkshake as a kid? This jam tastes great in a muffaletta and it makes a tuna salad sandwich infinitely more exciting.

4 cups pitted black olives, or a mix of black and green (about 2 pounds)

½ cup granulated sugar
½ cup packed light brown sugar

1. Rinse the olives under cold water and pat them dry. Put them in a blender or a food processor and process until they have broken down into a chunky puree, with olive bits the size of peas. (Or work them over with a knife if you're feeling like a hardbody.)

2. Put the olive puree in a small saucepan, stir in both sugars, and cook over medium-low heat, stirring, for 5 minutes. During that time, the sugars will melt, then begin to caramelize. Continue cooking until the mixture reaches a super-thick, jam-like consistency, about 15 minutes. Let cool.

3. Portion the jam out into jars. Keep refrigerated, and eat within 2 weeks.

This recipe will take whatever olive you've got: brined or cured, from a jar or canned; just make sure they're pitted.

TOMATO JAM

MAKES ABOUT 2 CUPS

This is a classic **tomato jam** with an Italian sauce twist: a little savory and a little sweet, just like Mamma used to make. Or maybe she didn't. But I know she'd like it.

4 pounds plum tomatoes, peeled, halved crosswise, seeded, and chopped

1 cup sugar

1 garlic clove, minced

⅛ teaspoon crushed red pepper flakes

1½ teaspoons kosher salt

⅛ teaspoon black pepper

⅛ teaspoon paprika

1 tablespoon chopped fresh oregano

1. Mix the tomatoes, sugar, garlic, and red pepper flakes in a large shallow nonreactive pot and bring the mixture to a boil over medium-high heat, stirring occasionally. Reduce the heat and boil, stirring often, until the tomatoes have softened and broken down, about 15 minutes.

2. Stir in the salt, pepper, paprika, and oregano and boil until the consistency of thick jam, about 10 minutes. Let cool.

3. Portion the jam out into jars. Keep refrigerated, and eat within 2 weeks.

To peel tomatoes with ease, with the sharp tip of a paring knife, cut an × into the bottom of each one. Blanch for 30 seconds in boiling water, shock (chill) in ice water, and then peel away.

SWEET-AND-SOUR RED ONION JAM

MAKES ABOUT 2 CUPS

Honestly, you don't need to put this jam on anything to enjoy it (I've caught houseguests eating it with their fingers straight out of the Tupperware container), although you certainly can: I rock my stock on a grilled cheese sandwich (see page 101), Seven-Layer Salad (page 20), or Eggs Benedict (page 232), or roll it inside some Haute Dogs (page 94).

4 small red onions

2 tablespoons vegetable oil

½ cup sugar

1 cup rice vinegar or champagne vinegar

2 teaspoons kosher salt

1. Peel the red onions and thinly slice into rings; use a mandoline if you've got one.

2. Heat the oil in a medium skillet over medium-low heat. Add the sliced onions and sweat until they begin to soften and turn translucent but do not brown, 10 to 15 minutes.

3. Add the sugar and vinegar and cook over *very* low heat until the liquid evaporates entirely and the jam is thick and sticky, about 10 minutes.

4. Take the jam off the heat and stir in the salt. Let cool.

5. Portion the jam out into jars. Keep refrigerated, and eat within 2 weeks.

COLD BREW

— MAKES 4 (12-OUNCE) CUPS OF COFFEE —

We make cold brew at Milk Bar throughout the spring, summer, and into the fall by steeping ground Stumptown coffee overnight in cold water. This process of "brewing" yields an incredibly smooth and highly potent yet gentle cup of less-acidic coffee, because the coffee never comes in contact with heat. I feel confident that it will be your new favorite way to make coffee, served at any temperature.

½ **pound** ground coffee, such as Stumptown (upscale) or Bustelo (supermarket style)

6 cups cold water

---

1. Stir together the coffee and water in a large pitcher. Cover the pitcher and refrigerate for at least 12, and as long as 15, hours.

2. Strain the cold brew through a fine-mesh sieve into another container. Then pour the strained coffee through a coffee filter back into the rinsed-out pitcher. Store in the fridge for up to a week.

To serve, decide if you'd prefer to drink it hot or cold. If you want hot coffee, put the coffee in a pan on the stovetop or in a cup in the microwave and heat it up. Don't let it boil! Dilute with water and/or milk to the desired strength.

CINNAMON BUNS

EARLY BIRDS

— MAKES 1 DOZEN BUNS —

When I was a teenager, my mother began a tradition of making cinnamon buns on special mornings when all the kids were home in the roost. When I became an unsalted-European-style-butter snob and pillowy dough fanatic, I revamped her recipe. I now run the stand mixer, and Mom has happily replaced me as the official taste tester. I make these delights for every houseguest; any excuse for a breakfast of cinnamon buns is a good one.

DEM BUNZ

1 cup whole milk, warmed

1 tablespoon warm water

1 packet (2¼ teaspoons) active dry yeast

4½ cups all-purpose or bread flour, plus more for dusting

½ cup granulated sugar

1 teaspoon kosher salt

1 large egg

1 large egg yolk

8 tablespoons (1 stick) unsalted butter, melted

DAT GOO

1 cup packed light brown sugar

5½ tablespoons unsalted butter, melted

2½ tablespoons ground cinnamon

½ teaspoon kosher salt

CREAM CHEESE FROSTING

3 ounces cream cheese, at room temperature

4 tablespoons (½ stick) unsalted butter, at room temperature

1½ cups confectioners' sugar

½ teaspoon vanilla extract

⅛ teaspoon kosher salt

1. Start with dem bunz: Whisk together the warm milk, water, and yeast in a small bowl. Let sit until foamy, 5 minutes or so.

2. Combine the flour, granulated sugar, and salt in the bowl of a stand mixer fitted with the dough hook and mix together on low speed. Add the egg, egg yolk, butter, and the yeast concoction and mix until the dough comes together as a thick, sticky mass. This should take 6 or so minutes. (For extra hardbody points, mix the dough by hand. It'll be messier but more satisfying.)

3. With a rubber spatula, scrape the dough out onto a work surface and form it into a smooth ball. Put that glorious ball into a greased-up bowl, seam side down, cover it with a kitchen towel, and set it in a draft-free spot (I like the microwave or a turned-off oven) to rise for an hour, or until it's doubled in size.

(recipe continues)

4. While the dough is rising, make dat goo: Mix together the brown sugar, butter, cinnamon, and salt in a small bowl.

5. Grab that proofed dough, punch it down, and put it on a well-floured counter. Use a rolling pin or wine bottle to roll it into a 16-inch square. Spread the cinnamon goo evenly over the surface, then roll the dough up into a big, tight tube, making sure to keep all the filling inside.

6. Using a sharp knife, slice the tube into 12 rounds, each about 1⅓ inches thick. Arrange the rounds cut side down in a 9 × 13-inch baking dish, leaving 1 inch between them. Let them rise for another 1 to 2 hours, until they've doubled in size.

7. Heat the oven to 375°F.

8. Bake the buns for 20 minutes, or until they are just starting to brown on the edges.

9. Meanwhile, make the cream cheese frosting: Combine the cream cheese and butter in the bowl of a stand mixer fitted with the paddle attachment and mix on high for 1 minute. Add the confectioners' sugar, vanilla, and salt and paddle on low to combine, then whip up a fury on high for 2 minutes, or until the frosting is a pale white and incredibly fluffy.

10. Remove the buns from the oven and, while they are still warm, spread the frosting generously over them. Serve immediately, and watch as they disappear before your very eyes.

If you don't have a 9 × 13-inch baking dish, you can use two smaller dishes, such as two 10-inch pie pans. Often I'll split the buns between a smallish baking dish and an aluminum pan—so I have some to keep and some to give away!

Night Owl this recipe and form the buns the night before. Let them rise, loosely covered, in the fridge overnight. All you'll need to do is take them out in the morning, let them come to room temp for about half an hour, and pop them in the oven.

POPOVERS

— MAKES 1 DOZEN BIG POPOVERS —

The name "popovers," like onomatopoeia but with action instead, describes what happens when these hollow delicacies are baked. The batter poofs up and pops over the rims of the muffin tin. Be prepared to hush your early-bird sleepover mates when they won't stop telling you how good they are.

They're also great fresh out of the oven with a bowl of soup for lunch or dinner.

3 **large** eggs
2 **large** egg whites
1¾ **cups** whole milk
1¾ **cups** all-purpose flour
2 **teaspoons** sugar
2 **teaspoons** kosher salt
¼ **teaspoon** black pepper

¼ **pound** Gruyère, Swiss, or any kind of cheese you got, shredded

> **For an easy take on a** sausage, egg, and cheese breakfast sandwich, prior to baking, add a sprinkling of chopped-up Jimmy Dean breakfast sausage to each batter-filled muffin cup with the cheese.

1. Heat the oven to 425°F. Grease a 12-cup muffin pan.

2. Measure all of the ingredients except the cheese into the pitcher of a blender. Blend on medium-low until smooth and well combined. The batter will be rather thin—don't panic.

3. Pour ⅓ cup batter into each cup. (Some people swear by preheating the muffin pan, but it's up to you. If it's too early in the morning, I never do.) Each cup should be a little more than half-full. Scatter the shredded cheese evenly over the center of the filled cups.

4. Put the popovers in the oven and bake for 30 to 40 minutes, until tripled in size, hollow in the center, and a healthy golden brown on the outside. You can stalk this process from the window of your oven, but DO NOT OPEN THE DAMN DOOR until they're done. Just don't. This is an extremely fragile process. Opening the oven will prevent your batter from popping over, and in turn, prevent these from fulfilling their life's purpose.

5. Pop out of the pan and dig in immediately. Popovers are best warm out of the oven, or the same day at the very latest. They will lose their crunchy, hollow magic if you attempt to save them for the next day.

TEX-MEX BREAKFAST CASSEROLE

— SERVES 6 TO 8 —

No one really wants to think about breakfast too much after staying up late making crafts and watching ridiculous movies from the early nineties. That's the best part about a breakfast casserole—you can pay it forward and whip it together in no time the night before, then warm it quickly the next a.m., and put it out on the table next to some spoons and plates, inviting your guests to graze and help themselves (after they've wiped off the messages you wrote on their foreheads and defrosted their bras).

There are two ways to approach this recipe: You can use frozen hash browns as the anchor element, or do what I do and use leftover Party Nachos (page 207). I always make too many nachos on purpose so I can use the leftovers to turn this casserole into a baller love letter to our favorite Austin dish, *migas*—essentially scrambled eggs and crispy tortilla chips.

---

1 (12-ounce) package breakfast sausage links

1 medium yellow onion, diced
1 jalapeño, diced

10 large eggs
1 cup cottage cheese or 4 ounces cream cheese, at room temperature
½ **cup** whole milk
¼ **cup** crumbled cotija cheese
½ **cup** shredded Monterey Jack or cheddar cheese

2½ **cups** leftover nachos or frozen shredded hash browns
kosher salt if using hash browns

½ **cup** shredded Monterey Jack or cheddar cheese

---

1. Heat the oven to 350°F.

2. Slice the sausage or remove it from the casings and cook in a skillet over medium heat until browned. Transfer the sausage to a large bowl, making sure to leave the rendered fat in the pan.

3. Add the onion and jalapeño to the pan and cook over medium-low heat until tender, about 10 minutes. Dump into the bowl of sausage.

4. Whisk together the eggs, cottage cheese, milk, cotija, and ½ cup Monterey Jack in a medium bowl.

5. Toss the leftover nachos into the sausage mixture, mix it all up, and spread the whole shebang evenly in a greased 9 × 13-inch baking dish (if using hash browns, season with 1 teaspoon salt before combining with the sausage mixture). Pour the egg and cheese mixture over it. Top with the remaining ½ cup Monterey Jack cheese.

6. Bake for 20 minutes, or until the casserole is golden brown and the eggs are set.

GOING OUT

You can't work in a restaurant without being obsessed with going *out* to restaurants. And, to be clear, I don't reserve eating out for special occasions. I eat out *often,* whether it's picking up a bag of tacos on my way home from a long day of work or going to wd~50 to check out Wylie's latest menu.

I call it "work" or "market research," but, really, going out is one of the lone yet great perks of living and working in New York City and being "in the biz." I have every type of cuisine at my fingertips, accessible at all hours of the day, and many of my favorite options even deliver directly to my apartment's Barcalounger, so I can eat out without going out.

The recipes in this chapter are an homage to my favorite dishes created by my favorite chefs at my favorite restaurants—hand-me-down adaptations of the most beloved and mind-blowingly delicious foods that I seek out when I venture from the bakery into the real world for a morning, noon, or night out on the town.

I make these recipes when I'm out of town visiting friends, on a family vacation, or want to throw a dinner party without ordering takeout to satisfy my craving, though the real thing is not to be missed either . . .

CORNBREAD ICE CREAM

— ADAPTED FROM SAM MASON AT ODDFELLOWS ICE CREAM CO. | MAKES 1 GENEROUS QUART —

Over a decade ago, I sought out a job at wd~50. I wanted to be part of the house of Wylie Dufresne, and I *needed* to work for Sam Mason. I was a huge fan of what pastry chefs Claudia Fleming and Karen DeMasco were doing with elevating classic down-home American desserts at the time, but I really wanted to tap into what Sam was doing at wd~50, turning classic American flavors inside out.

Sam breathed new life into the dessert world, pushing the boundaries of what dessert could be. He took classics like carrot cake, or even ants on a log, and picked them apart, only to put the flavors back together with new techniques and new meaning. This might read as a snooze today—you've heard of and/or tried all of these things before, but it's only because Sam revved up the revolution, yet gets very little credit. My career and Milk Bar's very existence owe a debt to both of them.

Nowadays Sam is running a fantastic old-timey ice cream shop on the Williamsburg waterfront, where he makes some of the best ice cream in New York. There you can score a peek at his handsome hair and a scoop of this cornbread ice cream, which I fell in love with as a pastry cook at wd~50 in 2005. It's sweet and savory and a great way to beat the heat on a hot summer day.

2 (8.5-ounce) boxes Jiffy corn muffin mix, baked according to the package directions

4 cups whole milk, plus more if needed

½ cup heavy cream

1 cup freeze-dried corn powder (find it at milkbarstore.com)

½ cup plus ⅓ cup nonfat milk powder

½ cup corn syrup

⅓ cup sugar

2 large eggs

½ teaspoon kosher salt

1. Heat the oven to 250°F.

2. Crumble the cornbread and spread the crumbles on a baking sheet. Toast the crumbs in the oven for about 20 minutes, rotating the pan halfway through baking, until golden brown and crouton-like in texture. Let cool completely.

Tempering is a pastry technique used when making custards that involve combining hot liquid with eggs. The trick to preventing the eggs from scrambling is to slowly pour the hot liquid into the eggs while whisking constantly to warm them gradually.

You can make the base a day or three ahead, but spin it right before you want to eat it. Ice cream always tastes best right out of the machine.

3. Put the cornbread crumbs in a large bowl and add the milk, heavy cream, and freeze-dried corn powder. Stir the ingredients and let steep for 10 minutes.

4. Strain the steeped mixture through a fine-mesh sieve into a bowl. Measure it: you need 3 cups of cornbread milk. If you do not have 3 cups, add more milk until you do. Discard the solids.

5. Pour 2 cups of the cornbread milk into a medium bowl and refrigerate. Pour the remaining 1 cup cornbread milk into a medium saucepan and heat over medium heat until hot to the touch, about 2 minutes, being careful not to scorch the bottom of the pot.

6. Meanwhile, whisk together the milk powder, corn syrup, sugar, eggs, and salt in a medium bowl until fully combined. When the cornbread milk is hot, slowly stream it into the egg mixture, whisking all the while so as not to scramble the eggs.

7. Pour the eggy milk back into the saucepan and continue whisking over medium heat until the mixture is hot to the touch and has thickened, about 1 minute. Remove from the heat and whisk the hot mixture into the bowl with the 2 cups cold cornbread milk. Refrigerate until cold, at least 30 minutes, or for up to 3 days.

8. Freeze the base in an ice cream machine according to the manufacturer's instructions.

EGGS BENEDICT WITH WYLIE'S HOLLANDAISE

— SERVES 6 —

I had never really contemplated making English muffins myself until I worked for Wylie Dufresne at wd~50 nearly a decade ago. That's where I became obsessed with experimenting my way into the perfect English muffin recipe. Why? Because Wylie subsists on a diet of American cheese, eggs, and hamburgers and he eats them *all* on Thomas' English muffins.

He's a huge fan of eggs Benedict ("What's cooler than eggs with egg sauce?" he will ask rhetorically), so I've interpreted that here with my homemade English muffin recipe and Wylie's formula for hollandaise sauce. One of his best-known restaurant dishes is a deconstructed eggs Benedict—slow-poached egg yolk, English-muffin-encrusted deep-fried hollandaise, and Canadian bacon chips—but neither you nor I will be making *that* at home.

Milk Bar English Muffins

12 cooked bacon slices, seared ham slices, or browned sausage patties
12 Soy Sauce Eggs (page 245), eggs for Egg Soup (page 122), or Poached Eggs (page 158)

Wylie's Hollandaise (page 234)
minced fresh chives (optional but nice)

1. Fork open the English muffins and put them in the toaster until lightly browned.

2. Put 2 English muffin halves onto each of six plates (make sure the plates are decorative; eggs Benedict is a *fancy* dish).

3. Top each muffin half with the protein of your choice, then top with the poached eggs. Spoon enough hollandaise sauce over each egg to fully cover it and drip down the sides of the English muffin onto the plate. For a lovely effect, sprinkle some chives on top of each dish. Serve immediately.

MILK BAR ENGLISH MUFFINS

MAKES 6 MUFFINS

2 teaspoons active dry yeast
1 tablespoon lukewarm water
½ **cup** buttermilk, warmed

1 cup bread flour, plus more for dusting
1 tablespoon sugar
1½ **teaspoons** kosher salt

1 tablespoon unsalted butter, at room
  temperature, plus more for the bowl

cornmeal for sprinkling

1. Whisk together the yeast and warm water in a medium bowl to dissolve the yeast. Whisk in the buttermilk, then transfer the mixture to the bowl of a stand mixer fitted with the dough hook.

2. Add the flour, sugar, and salt, turn the mixer on to low/medium-low, and mix just until it all comes together as a shaggy, droopy dough, 3 to 4 minutes.

3. With the mixer running, add the butter. The dough will look as if it is separating, and from this point on, it will hang out at the bottom of the bowl. Mix it for 7 to 8 minutes, by which time it should hold its shape and be tacky but no longer sticky.

4. Grease a large mixing bowl. Using a rubber spatula, transfer the dough to the bowl. Cover with plastic wrap and refrigerate for 1 hour, or as long as overnight; this makes the dough easier to handle.

5. Scatter a work surface and your hands with a fine dusting of flour. Turn the chilled dough out onto the work surface and knead it a few times to deflate it. Shape it into a fat, smooth-ish log. Divide said log into 6 equal pieces. With lightly floured palms, roll the pieces of dough into neat balls, applying as little pressure as possible, and transfer to a cornmeal-covered baking sheet, patting each dough ball down gently so some of the cornmeal adheres to the bottom. Gently flip

them over and pat them down again to get cornmeal on the other side as well. The tops and bottoms of the muffins should be covered with cornmeal, and the sides should be naked.

6. Make sure all the muffins have about an inch of space around them so they can proof properly. Wrap the baking sheet in plastic wrap and chill for 30 minutes.

7. Heat the oven to 250°F.

8. Warm a dry cast-iron skillet or griddle over the *lowest* heat possible for 5 or so minutes. You should be able to hold your hand very close to the pan and feel just a little radiant heat—nothing that would make you want to pull your hand back. Scatter the pan with a thin, even layer of cornmeal and warm for a minute more.

9. Transfer the cold proofed muffins to the warmed skillet—this is the all-important nook-and-crannies-forming stage of English muffin cookery: you want the muffins to rise and griddle-bake *slowly*. You almost can't take enough time with this stage. After about 4 minutes, the tops will begin to puff and dome (the undersides will also be a nice Thomas' English muffin brown)—that's your cue to flip them. Use a small offset spatula if you have one. After 4 or 5 minutes on the second side, using the same underbelly visual cue, transfer them to a clean baking sheet.

10. Put the muffins in the oven for 10 minutes to finish baking; the dough should look cooked through and not underbaked or soggy. Remove from the oven and let them cool completely on the baking sheet.

11. Use the fork method to separate the muffin into halves: Take a fork and stab the circumference of the muffin all the way around. The top should easily separate from the bottom.

WYLIE'S HOLLANDAISE

MAKES 2 CUPS

Heating the yolks over simmering water slowly cooks them while you emulsify them with the butter; if the water is too hot, or if you don't constantly whisk the yolks, you will end up with a greasy mess of scrambled eggs. Your arm will get tired, but be vigilant: don't stop whisking, and keep the water at just a simmer.

5 large egg yolks
1 to 2 tablespoons fresh lemon juice

½ pound (2 sticks) unsalted butter, melted and set aside in a bowl until the milk solids sink to the bottom

⅛ teaspoon cayenne pepper
1¼ teaspoons kosher salt
up to 2 tablespoons warm water

1. Fill a saucepan with 2 inches of water and bring to a simmer.

2. Whisk together like a maniac the egg yolks and 1 tablespoon lemon juice in a stainless steel bowl (one that will sit on the water-filled saucepan without touching the water) until the mixture is thick and voluminous. Set the bowl atop the saucepan (I repeat, the water should *not* touch the bottom of the bowl) and, whisking constantly, slowly drizzle in the melted butter, leaving the milk solids behind in the bottom of the bowl. The sauce will thicken and continue to gain volume.

3. Once all butter (sans solids) is drizzled and whisked in, remove from the heat and whisk in the cayenne and salt. Add additional lemon juice if you want it to be zingier. If the sauce gets thicker than you would like, whisk in up to 2 tablespoons warm water to loosen it.

4. Keep the hollandaise warm in your double boiler until ready to serve or for up to 20 minutes.

BANANA HAMMOCK PIZZA

— ADAPTED FROM ROBERTA'S | MAKES 2 INDIVIDUAL PIZZAS —

Even though Roberta's opened in Bushwick, Brooklyn, many years ago, the wait to get a table on any given night can still run up to three hours. (I order takeout when I'm in a hurry!) But I'm usually game to wait because the restaurant is more than just a pizza place—the rest of their food is super-delicious too. (They've got a handsome, red-covered cookbook out there on the shelves if you're interested in making more of it at home.)

The pizza is killer. It's partly the crust, with its perfect thickness and chewiness. And it's partly the toppings, which are very delicious and lead to hilarious names like the Cheesus Christ, the Little Stinker, and the Crispy Glover. My favorite Roberta's pizza is the Banana Hammock, topped with béchamel, mozzarella, pork sausage, garlic, red onion, banana peppers, red pepper flakes, and cilantro.

I love Roberta's because it challenges the notion of what a pizza topping is. This is much the way I approach pizza night at my apartment: fill up every bowl I own with delicious things, invite a bunch of people over, and wild out making our own combinations. Caramelized Leeks (page 160) with cinnamon and ricotta is clutch, as are, on any given pizza, Caramelized Onions (page 159), sesame seeds, and/or Poached Eggs (page 158).

The trick to a great pizza is to get the oven as hot as possible, 500° to 550°F. If you plan on making a lot of pizza, consider investing in a pizza stone—it will make the difference between a soggy crust and a crispy, browned beautiful piece of edible art, and it will get you as close as humanly possible to Roberta's wood-burning pizza oven. Even better? Throw that pizza on the grill. It will char the crust and lend a lovely, smoky flavor. For extra richness, drizzle the dough with a little olive oil before topping.

If you can't find banana peppers, any spicy long pepper is an acceptable substitute; jarred peperoncini work fine too.

THE CRUST

½ **teaspoon** active dry yeast
1 **cup** warm water
1 **teaspoon** olive oil

2½ **cups** bread flour
2 **teaspoons** kosher salt

cornmeal

THE BÉCHAMEL

1 **tablespoon** unsalted butter
1 **tablespoon** all-purpose flour
1 **cup** whole milk, warmed

½ **teaspoon** kosher salt
pinch of ground nutmeg

THE TOPPINGS

2 Italian sausages, casings removed
1½ **cups** shredded mozzarella
1 banana pepper, seeded and sliced
¼ **small** red onion, thinly sliced
6 garlic cloves, thinly sliced
½ **teaspoon** crushed red pepper flakes
small handful of fresh cilantro leaves

1. Make the crust: Stir together the yeast, water, and olive oil in a small bowl. Let sit for 3 minutes.

2. Combine the flour and salt in the bowl of a stand mixer fitted with the dough hook. Add the yeast mixture and mix on low until thoroughly combined, about 3 minutes. (If you're mixerless, you can do this by hand; just make sure everything is completely incorporated.) Let rest for 15 minutes in the mixing bowl.

3. Knead the dough on medium-low for 3 minutes longer, until it is smooth and springs back when poked. Let rest for 15 minutes more in the bowl.

4. Divide the dough in half and form into 2 balls. Put each ball in an oiled bowl and turn to coat. Cover each with a dampened cloth or towel and let rise at room temperature until roughly doubled in volume, 3 to 4 hours. (Alternatively, let rise in the refrigerator for 8 to 24 hours; allow to come to room temperature before baking.)

5. Make the béchamel: Melt the butter in a small saucepan over medium heat. Add the flour and whisk until smooth. Cook the mixture, stirring constantly, until it turns a sandy golden color, 3 to 4 minutes.

6. Stream the warm milk into the butter mixture, whisking until smooth. Bring to a boil and cook for 2 minutes, stirring constantly. Remove from the heat and season with the salt and nutmeg. Let the béchamel cool to room temperature; it will be thick but spreadable.

7. Position the rack close to your oven's heating element. Heat the oven to its highest temperature, 500° or 550°F; if you have a pizza stone, put it in the oven so it gets nice and toasty.

8. Brown the sausage: Cook the sausage in a small skillet over medium heat until it begins to crisp and brown, about 5 minutes. Set aside to cool.

9. Punch down the dough and roll out each piece into a 12-inch round. Sprinkle two baking sheets liberally with cornmeal. (If you are using a pizza stone, the baking sheets need to be rimless, or you can use the backs of rimmed ones.) Put one of the pizza rounds onto each baking sheet.

10. Spread half of the béchamel over each crust. Divvy up the mozzarella between the two and sprinkle the rest of the ingredients (sausage! pepper! red onion! garlic! red pepper flakes!) across the tops, forming clusters of toppings as you go.

11. When the oven is as hot as can be, bake the pizzas. Either slide onto the pizza stone one at a time or put the baking sheets in the oven. Bake until the cheese begins to bubble and the crust is golden brown, 7 to 8 minutes. Sprinkle the cilantro evenly over the pizzas, slice, and serve.

KALE SALAD

— ADAPTED FROM BROOKLYN STAR | SERVES 4 —

Joaquin Baca (or Quino, as anyone who knows the handsome devil calls him) is, like many in the Milk Bar circle of life, a TEXAN. He helped open and shape Momofuku in the early years before moving to Brooklyn to open his own spot and serve the food he loves most. The straightest shooter I know, Quino comforts hearts and stomachs at the Brooklyn Star, challenging classics like fried chicken, biscuits, and collard greens to the soulful stylings of Johnny Cash, Willie Nelson, and Loretta Lynn, before driving his beat-up '79 rust-blue Datsun pickup home each night.

Kale has been the vegetable du jour for many jours at this point. What I once thought was the latest food trend has turned into a classic and is here to stay because of dishes like Brooklyn Star's kale salad. The raisins add a sweet element and, with the spicy peanuts, make a salad that's reminiscent of a PB & J sandwich, one of very few ways to get me to eat a salad.

THE RAISINS

1 cup golden raisins

2 cups apple cider

THE CHEDDAR CRISPS

1 cup shredded cheddar cheese

THE PEANUTS

2 tablespoons honey

2 teaspoons chili powder

1 cup roasted peanuts

1 tablespoon cider vinegar

1 tablespoon olive oil

THE KALE

1 bunch (about ¾ pound) black kale, the spicier the better

THE DRESSING

4 lemons, juiced

½ cup olive oil

1 teaspoon kosher salt

½ teaspoon black pepper

1. Prep the raisins: Combine the raisins with the apple cider in a small saucepan and simmer over medium heat until plumped and doubled in size, about 20 minutes. Let the raisins cool in the cooking liquid for at least 10 minutes to soak up additional liquid.

2. Drain the raisins in a sieve set over a bowl. Reserve ⅓ cup of the liquid and let both cool.

3. Heat the oven to 250°F.

4. Prep the cheddar crisps: Sprinkle the shredded cheddar in a thin layer on a baking sheet and bake, rotating the pan every 10 minutes, until the cheese is browned, dried out, and crispy. Be patient—this can take up to an hour, depending on the moisture level of the cheese. Let the cheese cool completely, then break it up into small shards. Turn the oven up to 300°F.

5. Prep the peanuts: Combine the honey and chili powder in a small bowl, add the peanuts, and toss to coat. Stir in the cider vinegar and olive oil. Spread out on a greased baking sheet and bake for 10 to 12 minutes, until dark brown. Remove from the oven.

6. Prep the kale: Stem the kale and remove the tough center ribs. Slice the leaves crosswise into thin strips, then crush the strips with your hands, softening and bruising the greens so they're ready to soak up the dressing.

7. Make the dressing: Combine the lemon juice with the reserved apple cider in a big salad bowl. Drizzle in the olive oil, whisking constantly to emulsify, then add the salt and pepper. Add the raisins and peanuts.

8. Add the kale and toss with a pair of tongs to make sure everything gets coated evenly. Top the salad with the cheddar cheese crisps and serve.

ZUCCHINI PARM

— ADAPTED FROM NO. 7 SUB | MAKES 1 (6-INCH) SUB —

I love me a good sandwich. Though I can be a purist at times—I'll take a turkey club or a perfectly executed BLT when the mood strikes—nothing draws me in and impresses me more than a clever sandwich construction. Tyler Kord from No. 7 Sub has a knack for challenging what can be slathered on bread or stuffed in between. All of his sandwiches are damn delicious to boot, and they inspire my creativity and boundary-challenging, rule-breaking mentality with every bite. The Zucchini Parm is my favorite, for its left-field ingredients combo that works, coupled with the fact that anyone willing to stuff BBQ potato chips into a sandwich has my devotion for life.

For a healthier but still quite delicious version of this sandwich, bake the zucchini instead of frying it. Heat the oven to 350°F, arrange the breaded zucchini on a baking sheet, and bake until brown and crispy, 15 to 20 minutes.

THE ZUCCHINI PARM

1 medium zucchini
½ teaspoon kosher salt

2 large eggs
1 cup all-purpose flour

1 cup plain dried bread crumbs
½ teaspoon paprika
½ teaspoon kosher salt
½ teaspoon black pepper

grapeseed oil for shallow-frying

THE ASSEMBLY

1 (6-inch) sub roll, sliced lengthwise in half
2 slices Fontina cheese
1 tablespoon mayonnaise, preferably Kewpie
1½ tablespoons Sweet-and-Sour Red Onion Jam (page 215)
2 tablespoons sliced pickled jalapeños
handful of BBQ chips

1. Prep the zucchini Parm: Using a mandoline or a sharp knife, slice the zucchini lengthwise into ¼-inch-thick strips (i.e., not into coins). Put the strips on a baking sheet and sprinkle on both sides with the salt. (This will draw out excess moisture and prevent the zucchini from becoming soggy.) Let stand for 15 to 20 minutes; soon you'll see liquid beading up on the strips.

2. Heat the oven to 375°F. Line a baking sheet with parchment or a kitchen towel.

3. Meanwhile, beat the eggs in a medium bowl. Dump the flour into a shallow bowl. Combine the bread crumbs, paprika, salt, and pepper in a third bowl.

4. Time to dredge! Dry off the zucchini strips with a paper towel. Dunk each strip first in the flour, then in the egg, back in the flour, the egg again, and then the bread crumbs, ensuring an even coating of each layer at each stage, and set the breaded strips on the baking sheet as you go.

5. Heat ½ inch of oil to 350°F in a medium skillet. Gently lower the strips in, 2 to 3 per batch, and fry, turning once, until deep brown and crisp, about 3 minutes per side. Transfer to a paper-towel-lined plate.

6. While the strips are frying, lay the 2 halves of the roll open face up on a baking sheet. Put the Fontina on one side, fully covering it. Put both halves of the roll in the oven and toast until the cheese has melted, about 2 minutes. Remove from the oven.

7. Squirt the Kewpie mayo on the non-cheese side of your toasted roll. Top with the red onion jam. Lay down the strips of zucchini and pile on the jalapeños and BBQ chips. Press down to mush everything together. Eat while still warm.

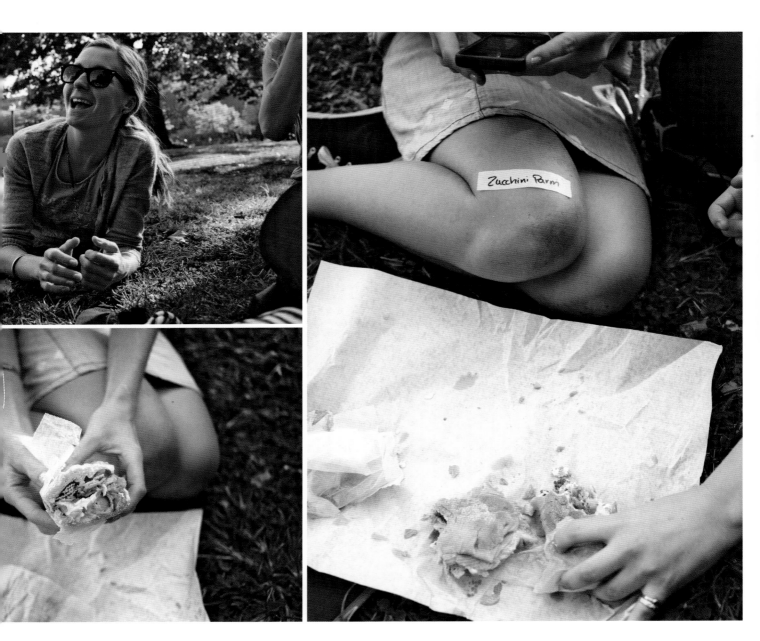

Zucchini Parm

AREPAS DE PABELLÓN

— ADAPTED FROM CARACAS RESTAURANT | MAKES 6 AREPAS —

A classic Venezuelan flatbread made of cornmeal, arepas speak to my down-home, country-cooking side. Essentially griddled corn cakes, they remind me of a cross between a crunchy taco and a pita pocket, and they are the perfect vessel for any filling you can imagine.

The arepa dough can be a little tricky to master, but once you do, it will be one of those things to keep hidden up your sleeve to bust out and impress everyone.

I limit myself to a once-a-week visit to the fine establishment in the East Village. I order the same thing every time, the *de pabellón* arepa, with the most classic filling: shredded beef, fried sweet plantains, black beans, and cotija, a salty white cheese. Here is my version.

THE AREPA DOUGH

1½ cups lukewarm water, plus more if needed

2 teaspoons kosher salt

1 cup masarepa (precooked white corn flour), plus more if needed

1 tablespoon grapeseed or other neutral oil

cornmeal for dusting
nonstick cooking spray

THE BEEF

1 tablespoon grapeseed or other neutral oil

½ medium Spanish onion, chopped

1 red bell pepper, cored, seeded, and chopped

1 jalapeño pepper, seeded and chopped

6 garlic cloves

1 (4-ounce) can tomato paste

2 tablespoons Worcestershire sauce

1 cup leftover Bo Ssäm Challenge liquid (page 104)

1 pound shredded cooked beef or Bo Ssäm Challenge brisket (page 104)

THE PLANTAINS

½ cup grapeseed or other neutral oil

1 ripe plantain, sliced ¼ inch thick on the bias

kosher salt

THE ASSEMBLY

½ cup Bean Dip (page 174)

¼ cup crumbled cotija cheese

Masarepa is precooked cornmeal made specifically with arepas in mind, and it is an essential ingredient—no substitutions please! Latin grocery stores sell it. So does the internet.

If you don't have any reserved cooking liquid from the Bo Ssäm brisket, use 1 cup water or beef or chicken stock plus 1 teaspoon sugar and salt to taste as a substitute.

If you don't feel like making bean dip (for shame!), empty a 15-ounce can of black beans into a pot, heat them on the stove until they are hot, and use them instead.

1. Prep the arepa dough: Stir together the warm water and salt in a large bowl to dissolve the salt. Gradually add the masarepa, mixing with your fingers to dissolve any lumps; if necessary, add additional masarepa to make a soft dough that holds its shape without cracking. Let the dough rest for 3 minutes.

2. Add the oil to the dough and work it in with your hands, adding more masarepa or water as necessary. There should be little to no cracking; this is a very soft dough.

3. Divide the dough into 6 equal portions. Shape each into a 1-inch-thick disk, 3 to 4 inches in diameter. Transfer to a baking sheet dusted with cornmeal, so the arepas don't stick.

4. Heat the oven to 350°F.

5. Spray a large nonstick skillet or griddle with cooking spray and warm it over medium heat. Put the arepas in the skillet, in batches, and griddle until the underside is a splotchy golden brown, about 4 minutes. Using a spatula, flip them and brown the other side in the same manner. Return to the baking sheet.

6. When all of the arepas are browned, transfer them directly to an oven rack (without the baking sheet). Bake until the surface of the arepas has formed a taut skin—if you rap your fingers on one, it should feel and sound like a little drum—about 10 minutes. Return the arepas to the baking sheet and let them cool slightly.

7. Meanwhile, prep the beef: Heat the oil in a large sauté pan over medium-high heat. Add the onion, bell pepper, jalapeño, and garlic and cook until softened, about 10 minutes. Stir in the tomato paste and cook for 3 minutes to evaporate the juices slightly. Add the Worcestershire sauce, Bo Ssäm Challenge liquid, and meat, bring to a simmer, and simmer for 5 minutes. Remove from the heat.

8. Prep the plantains: Heat the grapeseed oil in a large pan over medium-high heat, to 350°F. Add the plantains and shallow-fry them, turning once, until they are browned and soft, about 3 minutes per side. Remove the plantains from the oil with a slotted spoon and lay them on a paper-towel-lined plate or tray. Sprinkle lightly with salt.

9. Assemble: With a knife, split each arepa halfway open, and then hollow out a little of the soft innards to make room for the filling. Stuff the hollowed-out arepa shells with the shredded beef, plantain slices, beans, and cotija cheese. Eat warm.

SOY SAUCE EGGS

— ADAPTED FROM MOMOFUKU NOODLE BAR | MAKES 6 EGGS

This super-simple recipe from Momofuku Noodle Bar is one of my favorites in this book. At the restaurant, the eggs are halved, seasoned with Maldon salt and black pepper, and garnished with fried shallots and chives. But— important here—the eggs can also be used in a thousand different ways: they are perfect on their own as a snack, or on an English muffin (eggs Benny setup), in pasta, or cut up and mixed into a salad. The egg white soaks up the flavor of the soy sauce and the yolk is cooked perfectly, just a little bit runny and viscous enough to cling to whatever you serve it with. If you aren't sure what to use them for, just make a batch and keep them in your fridge. You'll find yourself putting them on or in everything.

6 tablespoons warm water
1 tablespoon sugar
2 tablespoons sherry vinegar
¾ **cup** soy sauce

6 large eggs
Maldon or other flaky sea salt
black pepper

1. Whisk together the water and sugar in a medium bowl to dissolve the sugar, then stir in the sherry vinegar and soy sauce.

2. Bring a large pot of water to a boil. Carefully put the eggs into the boiling water and cook for exactly 6 minutes and 50 seconds, stirring slowly for the first 1½ minutes to distribute the heat evenly. Use a timer! Meanwhile, fill a large bowl with cold water and ice. When the timer rings, transfer the eggs to the ice bath.

3. Once they are cool, peel the eggs (in the ice water—this helps ensure a porcelain-like exterior). Transfer the peeled eggs to the soy sauce mixture and marinate in the fridge for at least 2, or up to 6, hours, making sure they are completely submerged; if necessary top the eggs with a small plate to ensure submersion.

4. Remove the eggs from the sweet-and-salty solution (you can save this for another go next week). The eggs will keep in the fridge for up to a month.

5. To serve, cut the eggs lengthwise in half and season with sea salt and pepper. Or *Cool Hand Luke* them to impress your friends.

MAC-'N-CHEESE PANCAKES

— ADAPTED FROM SHOPSIN'S | SERVES 4 —————————————

Shopsin's is a little cubbyhole in NYC's Essex Street Market. Its owner, Kenny Shopsin, has created the most insane menu I've ever seen; it has around nine hundred items, each relevant in its own right. Most people are scared of Kenny, as he tends toward crabbiness. He's a very no-nonsense guy when it comes to overly enthusiastic guests in his joint. Me, I love the guy. He wears it on his sleeve. I do my best to keep it cool.

It's overwhelming having to choose what to order, wonderful to contemplate how the heck such a ginormous menu comes out of such a tiny, open kitchen, and a special pleasure to have Kenny stink-eye you all the while. I tell people that if they just can't decide, they should (1) not make eye contact with Kenny and (2) order the mac-'n-cheese pancakes. They are perfect for breakfast, lunch, or dinner and can be served with sweet or savory accoutrements. They're also delicious when eaten in fear.

If you're interested in the full Shopsin's story, check out the documentary I Like Killing Flies *and the book* Eat Me: The Food and Philosophy of Kenny Shopsin.

1 cup all-purpose flour

2 tablespoons freeze-dried corn powder (find it at milkbarstore.com)

2 tablespoons sugar

2 teaspoons baking powder

1 teaspoon kosher salt

1 cup whole milk

1 large egg

3 tablespoons grapeseed or other neutral oil

2 cups cheesy mac-'n-cheese

Use your favorite mac-'n-cheese for this recipe, whether it's a treasured family recipe or a box of Kraft. It doesn't matter; the 'cakes will be delicious either way. But please be sure to stir a tablespoon or two of shredded sharp cheddar cheese into the prepared mac. The cheesier the better.

1. Whisk together the flour, corn powder, sugar, baking powder, and salt in a medium bowl.

2. Whisk together the milk, egg, and oil in a small bowl. Pour into the flour mixture and whisk until your pancake batter is even and smooth; be careful not to overmix.

3. Heat a griddle or nonstick skillet over medium heat. Work in 2 batches and make 2 pancakes at a time: Pour ¼ cup batter onto the griddle for each pancake and top each with ¼ cup mac-'n-cheese. Use your fingers to spread the mac evenly throughout the batter, then cook until the pancake batter has set on the bottom and browned (bubbles will begin to appear on the top and a few will burst), 1 to 2 minutes. Flip carefully with a thin spatula and then cook the other side until golden brown, 1 to 2 minutes.

4. Serve warm. I like to roll my pancakes up into a taquito or flauta-like shape to eat with ease.

Serve these pancakes as you make them or keep them warm in a 200°F oven and serve them all at once.

BRISKET AND BROCCOLI

— ADAPTED FROM MISSION CHINESE | SERVES 4 TO 6 —

Mission Chinese's brisket and broccoli (Danny Bowien's play on the classic Chinese beef and broccoli) is one of the reasons folks wait for hours to score a table in the red-lit back room of his NYC eatery. I call in an order and pick up my food at the door, next to the keg, because mama don't mess with that. I leave a trail of cookies, throw my boy a high five, and run.

This dish is sweet, salty, and beefy, and it has broccoli in it. (I often whisper to myself in the bathroom mirror in the morning, Please, please, please, Christina. Try to eat something green today, OK?) Mission Chinese accomplished!

THE BRISKET

6 ounces leftover Bo Ssäm Challenge brisket (page 104), pastrami, or corned beef
¼ cup yellow mustard

THE SAUCE

⅓ cup soy sauce
1 tablespoon Asian sesame oil
1 tablespoon light brown sugar
2 teaspoons oyster sauce
⅛ teaspoon liquid smoke

THE SLURRY

1½ teaspoons cornstarch
1½ teaspoons water

THE BROCCOLI

½ pound Chinese broccoli

1 tablespoon grapeseed or other neutral oil

1 tablespoon chopped garlic

1 teaspoon sesame seeds

1. Heat the oven to 220°F.

2. Prep the brisket: Put the brisket in a small baking dish and rub with the yellow mustard. Cover with foil and bake for 10 minutes, so the mustard penetrates the meat. Slice against the grain into slices about ½ inch thick.

3. Prep the sauce: Mix the soy sauce, sesame oil, brown sugar, oyster sauce, and liquid smoke in a small bowl.

4. Prep the slurry: Mix the cornstarch and water in a small bowl (a tiny bowl, if you have one) until smooth.

If you aren't a total salt-head, you may find this recipe to be a little on the salty side. In that case, feel free to substitute 1 tablespoon water for 1 tablespoon of the soy sauce.

The cornstarch and water mixture is called a slurry, a classic way of thickening sauces. The cornstarch is mixed with cold water before adding it to keep it from getting lumpy.

Chinese-style wok cooking comes at you hot and fast. Have all of your mise-en-place ready to go, because once you start cooking, there's no time to stop. If you step away, you're gonna burn something.

5. Prep the broccoli: Bring a medium saucepan of water to a boil. Slice the broccoli on an extreme bias into 1/4-inch-thick slices and blanch it in the boiling water for 1 minute. Drain in a colander and immediately cool it by running cold water over it. Drain well and pat the broccoli dry.

6. Time to cook: Heat the grapeseed oil in a wok or large heavy-bottomed sauté pan over high heat. When it sends up a whisper of smoke, add the meat and cook for about 20 seconds, stirring and shaking the pan, until the meat is coated in oil and beginning to sizzle. Add the garlic and stir until it just begins to brown, about 10 seconds. Add the broccoli and stir-fry for about 10 seconds, then add the soy sauce mixture and cook, stirring constantly, for about 1 minute.

7. Stir in the cornstarch slurry, bring the liquid to a boil, and boil for 20 to 30 seconds, until the sauce thickens.

8. Pour the contents of the pan onto a serving plate, sprinkle the top with sesame seeds and, quick! serve! Or put in a Chinese take-out box and bring to your friend's house.

TELLING IT LIKE IT IS:
MILK BAR TERMINOLOGY

We always have fun at Milk Bar, and we turn almost everything into a joke. Laughter keeps us going. For example, when it's the middle of the holidays, and it's 3 a.m., and we are still at work packing cookies into tins for the Union Square Holiday Market, and we know we will only get three hours of sleep before we have to start another heinously long workday, someone will sing out, "BOOM BOOM BOOM!" (see below) and we'll all crack up. Laughter always gives us that last bit of energy we need to make it through.

We are big fans of acronyms and making up silly names for things. It makes us feel like we're in the coolest (uncool) clique and in on a secret that no one else has a clue or cue to. We pretty much have a whole Milk Bar language at this point. It's all about celebrating the Everyday Ordinary. It's the Milk Bar way of life.

BOOM BOOM BOOM!
This is an oft-used phrase among a select group of the Milk Bar management team. We say it loudly and often. It's our personal Tourette's that we sing or scream, in the cadence of the Outhere Brothers' hit single, to break the silence, smooth over the insanity, and reduce stress.

Ask five milk maids or men about when one might use this ditty, and I can guarantee you, no answer will match up with another—but that's beside the point.

BOX KICKING

We end up with a lot of empty cardboard boxes. We always break them down and recycle them, but, every once in a while, you know what we like to do before we break them down? Kick the *cuss* out of them. It's a great stress reliever and really cathartic. It's also the liveliest of entertainment. Donkey-kick one for bonus points.

CHIPPINS
See *Dippins*.

CHOOSE YOUR OWN ADVENTURE

Once you know how to think about food and approach it with solid techniques, you can really get the job done with as much or as little as you have to cook with. I'd love it if you followed these recipes to a tee, but sometimes even I don't follow my recipes. Sometimes I just go into my cupboards and go from there. It's like grabbing a book from R. A. Montgomery's luminous series. Nothing wrong with approaching life like you're six or seven again. Once I know the parameters of a recipe, I'll swap things in and out. Approach the kitchen with a sense of adventure and excitement about trying new things. That's how to translate yourself into the food you're making. It's also often how

we get family meal on the table—e.g., "I'll poach eggs and we can set out buns for people to choose-your-own-adventure their sandwiches."

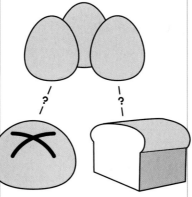

A CUSS-TON
A cuss-ton is an obscene amount of something, but way more lady-like.

DEAR DIARY

Listen: there is a large percentage of women at Milk Bar. And as women, we like to henpeck, chat, blabber, and gossip. When one of us needs a sounding board to get the crazies out of our head and the frustration off our chest, we "Dear Diary" someone. This usually involves going into way more detail than needed to get the point across, as you would in your teenage diary. But the days are long and we've got time, so this is an essential part of making it through a busy shift. It's also how we know what's going on in each

other's lives—and gain much fodder for inside jokes.

DIPPINS

"Dippins" is a funny way to refer to dips. It's funny because it rhymes with chippins, or chips. And people sound ridiculous when they refer to chips and dips as chippins and dippins. Try getting all your friends to start saying it. Then make fun of them.

DOUBLE TAP

If one of us sees somebody doing something that we firmly disagree with—taking so much family meal that there's not enough for the rest of the clan is a classic example—we go up to them and give 'em a firm double tap on the shoulder and tell them to stop. It's extremely important that the taps are strong yet short in duration and that there are only two.

Everyone needs a double tap once in awhile. You might even have to double tap yourself. You might have to double tap the person who gets in your way even though you've yelled out, "Hot pan!" You might have to double tap the person eating all the chocolate chips when you're trying to make cornflake chocolate chip marshmallow cookies. To be clear: you don't actually have to physically double tap someone, as long as you confront them and tell them what's what. Straighten up. Be concise yet direct. Get the point across quickly. No passive aggression allowed.

THE MILK BAR SWEAT DOWN

The Milk Bar sweat down occurs most often when we are getting the runaround. I'm not blind. We're a pretty young group of mostly gals running a pretty large company. We have sweet voices and wear colorful scarves on our heads. We make cookies for a living. For some reason, this often leads to grown-ups, mostly men, thinking they can play us. *Not so.* We weren't born yesterday, and we've fought for everything we have. We know how to blow out a compressor, clean out a grease trap, and change the oil in our delivery truck too. There's no way in heck we're going to let anyone take advantage, steal a penny they didn't earn, or slip one by us. We've perfected the essence of following up, following through, and, at all costs, sweating any given person down. I will call you every five minutes until eternity if you have not returned my phone call about a quote on a broken oven thermostat, an invoice adjustment, or a promise made. I will research online and fib to the receptionist until I reach the president of your company to make sure the place I built and people I lead are treated fairly and protected. And you will sweat it out if you choose to try and treat me any less than fairly.

OG

Original Gangster! Old Goodie! If something is OG, it's the original—the first of its kind. It was also the fourth album by Ice T. We use "OG," a lot, to refer to classic techniques and ingredients, and to pay our respects to either.

POLITE IGNORE

Much like a polite no (see below), the polite ignore is saved for those we simply cannot make contact with or respond to without being impolite. Rather than rolling our eyes, having a fit, or saying something mean, we button it up and remember we were raised by stand-up ladies and men.

POLITE NO

We get *a lot* of e-mail inquiries. People ask us to participate in events, to teach a class, to open a new storefront in a remote location, to do almost anything under the sun. Although I wish we could, we just can't say yes to everything; it's not humanly possible. When someone sends us an inquiry that I would *love* to say yes to, but can't, my staff and I always reply with a polite no. This term has seeped into our lives outside of work too. When you're Dear Diary-ing up a tale about a day-off adventure, more often than not, it's about how you had to polite-no the heck out of a situation, confrontation, or pickup attempt.

T-BALLED

Succeeding in the kitchen is all about setting yourself up for success. Think about the classic American game of T-ball: putting a ball on a stand at the exact right height and leaving it there for your teammate to step up to the plate and knock that ball right out of the park! In the Milk Bar kitchen, it's a compliment when someone says, "Wow! You just T-balled that!" Sometimes a high five or an attempted chest bump ensues. You get the picture. You can do the same in your home kitchen by reading through a recipe and having all of your ingredients ready before you start.

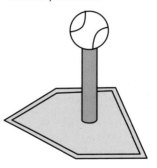

TERMS OF ENDEARMENT

The Russian language is filled with diminutives (*ichka* and *ovka,* for example), as is Spanish (*ita* and *ito* are a few). I have some of my own. I love shortening people's names and/or adding an *ini,* or just a *y.* Martine becomes Martini, Walter becomes Walty. I almost never refer to people by their proper names; it seems stiff and too serious for the kind of work we're doing. (And if anyone calls me Christina, I give them the stink-eye. It's Tos, or I don't answer.) When nothing else will do, I stick with Mama. It never gets old, and it always warms my heart and theirs.

THANKS

To my Milk Bar family: There are too many of you to name, but not a single one of you is possible to forget (especially after the Cookie a Day photo shoot). Since we opened six years ago, I can still count on my hands and toes the number of days I've taken off from work. Every other day has been spent with you, happily and honorably. It would never be worth it if it were not for each and every one of you. You've challenged who I am as a person, as a leader, as a creative mind, as a(n) (im)patient, penny-pinching, sometimes-too-serious work mom, reminding me that there is no limit, only challenge, with all things life throws my way.

To the cookbook family: Courtney McBroom, Peter Meehan, Gabriele Stabile, Mark Ibold, Ryan Healey, Walter Green, and Jason Polan. Thanks for believing, for putting up with the ridiculous concoctions and concepts that spurred this project, and for taking yet another leap of faith in tempering harebrained ideas and transforming them into something real. You T-balled the heck out of this one! (It is also NO fun doing the work without you.)

To Kim Witherspoon, for guiding, advising, and force-fielding me from the real world.

To the gals at Clarkson Potter: Rica Allannic, for her virtuous patience, enthusiasm, and care, even when all I gave her were excuses. Judith Sutton, for her meticulous copyediting—I'm convinced she's a superhero living among us. Marysarah Quinn, for her open-mindedness and design direction. Christine Tanigawa, Kim Tyner, Erica Gelbard, Kevin Sweeting, Doris Cooper, and Aaron Wehner, for their support.

To Dave Chang, though not understanding it whatsoever, for embracing my approach to life, and giving me the stage to share it the Milk Bar way.

To my blood: parents, siblings, aunts and uncles, grandparents, cousins, half-cousins—the whole kit and caboodle. You brought me into life and taught me how to live it first. You were my first and will remain my last line of defense when I choose to live it like a maniac. Thank you for always making home a place of acceptance, understanding, love, trips to the supermarket, feasts of fancy (OK, never, ever fancy), and rides from the train station late at night. When the next generation comes into their own, you can be sure they'll always have a summer job and a forever young, freakishly old auntie in me to guide them.

To my makeshift family, past and present, for spicing up life and teaching me home can be where I lay my head as long as it's near one of you: the Bignellis, the Wachsstocks, the Miller Williams clan, the Basils, the Stupaks.

To Joshua and Beans. You are all things blood to makeshift family to Milk Bar family. Thank you for mudding, constructing, complaining about, and challenging life on my terms and for the ideas, inspiration, and sacrifice of being my honorary guinea pigs at suppertime for so many years. Go out and get that world! (I've always got your back.)

To Tina, Amanda, and Chela, for reaffirming the fact that fancy, hardworking women *can* make a soft-boiled egg with toast points every bit as classy and chic as a five-star meal.

To Ken Friedman and his big green egg in MTK.

To the future, for the endlessly exciting things (and people) it surely holds each day. Don't forget to slow your roll for just a second, let your guard down, and do something utterly ridiculous like leap into a game of double Dutch, knot up a crafty friendship bracelet on the fly, logroll down a hill in your three-piece suit, or get unreasonably dolled up and go to the supermarket for something as simple as a red onion—that sweet-and-sour jam is always sure to come with a good backstory.

INDEX